HEAVENLY ADVANCE

PROPHETIC INTERCESSION

ACTIVATING THE FORCES OF GOD'S ANGELIC ARMIES

Jeanette Strauss

2020 © Jeanette Strauss

This book is protected under the copyright laws of the United States of America. All rights reserved. This book may not be copied or reprinted for commercial gain or profit. The use of short quotations or occasional page copying for personal or group study is permitted and encouraged. Permission will be granted upon request.

Unless otherwise noted Scriptures used are from the Amplified® Bible, Copyright © 1954,1958, 1962, 1964, 1965, 1987 by The Lockman Foundation. Used by permission.

Scripture marked NLT are taken from the Holy Bible, New Living Translation, copyright ©1996, 2004, 2007, 2013, 2015 by Tyndale House Foundation. Used by permission of Tyndale House Publishers, Inc. Carol Stream, Illinois 60188. All rights reserved.

Scriptures marked NKJV are from the New King James Version Bible. Copyright 1982 by Thomas Nelson Inc. Used by permission.

Scriptures marked NRSV from the New Revised Standard Version Bible, copyright © 1989 the Division of Christian Education of the National Council of the Churches of Christ in the United States of America. Used by permission. All rights reserved.

Scriptures marked ESV are from The ESV® Bible (The Holy Bible, English Standard Version®). ESV® Text Edition: 2016. Copyright © 2001 by Crossway, a publishing ministry of Good News Publishers.

I have purposely used the scriptures from the Amplified Bible and the New Living Translation Bible because they are easily understood, and this book is meant to be as easy to understand as possible, whether you are new to this type of ministry or a veteran prophetic intercessor.

Text marked *Commentary* is commentary taken from the New Spirit-Filled Life Bible, Copyright 2002 by Thomas Nelson, Inc. Used by permission.

Please note that the name "satan" and all names related to him are not capitalized. I have made a conscious decision not to capitalize his name, even to the point of violating grammar rules.

Published by *Glorious Creations Publications*: www.gloriouscreations.net

ISBN 13 978-0-9907742-2-8

Cover by James Nesbit, Prepare the Way Ministries, International

www.ptwministries.com

Table of Contents

Introduction 1

1 The Ministry of Intercession 3

2 The Purpose of Prophetic Intercession 19

3 Prophetic Intercession -- Relationship not Religion 33

4 Ways to Receive the Prophetic Word of the Lord 43

5 The Lord Speaks the Language of Symbolism 63

6 Prophetic Dreams and Visions 77

7 Prophetic Artisans 99

8 We Remember— Then We Demonstrate! 111

9 Prophetic Intercession with Angelic Intervention 119

10 What Kind of People Are Prophetic Intercessors? 135

Introduction

The focus of this book is prophetic intercession and the interaction of the angelic host in response to this type of intercession.

We can identify ways that God has instructed His people to intercede throughout history, by reading what has been recorded in the Bible. You will read examples of prophetic intercessors and the ways they expressed their prayers following God's directions.

As we read the results of their prophetic demonstrations, it attests to the reliability of the scriptures promoting this form of "God's way of thinking" intercession.

As ordinary people obediently followed God's instructions, even though what He was asking them to do seemed to be humanly impossible, miracles happened. Many of those miracles record that the Lord dispatched heavenly host angels to assist the person in accomplishing His purposes on the earth.

As we read about these historical events we will be encouraged to interact with God as they did, and to listen to what He is telling us to do and then act in faith to fulfill His instructions.

> Trust in the Lord with all of your heart and lean not unto your own understanding. In all your ways acknowledge him and he will direct your path. Proverbs 3:5-6 NIV

Our lives and our actions may even be linked to ancient prophesies appointed to be fulfilled through us in our time.

We may think that what He asks us to do is challenging or even impossible, but by studying the past we learn to expect the unexpected from God, and we train ourselves to look forward to following His instructions by faith and expecting the miraculous.

The great people of faith in the Bible must have questioned some of His instructions, but they trusted God and acted out of obedience to perform whatever it was He told them to do. We are only required to do our part and the Lord will take care of the rest. We listen. We act. He acts.

> *By faith Noah, when warned about things not yet seen, in Godly fear built an ark to save his family. By faith he condemned the world and became heir of the righteousness that comes by faith.*
> *Hebrews 11:7*

As we act in faith trusting God, we too will perform great exploits.

> *...those who know their God shall be strong and do mighty exploits. Daniel 11:32b*

As you read this book, your spiritual vision will be enhanced and you will be better able to relate to the value of the use of prophetic intercession. My prayer is that no matter what stage of life you are in, or whatever your spiritual upbringing has been, you will find information that will be an asset to you in your walk as a believer.

Chapter 1

The Ministry of Intercession

The Bible exhorts all believers to be intercessors

I exhort therefore, that, first of all, supplications, prayers, intercessions, and giving of thanks, be made for all men; For kings, and for all that are in authority; that we may lead a quiet and peaceable life in all godliness and honesty.
1 Timothy 2:1-2 KJV

This scripture is a call to action from God for intercession. It is addressed to every believer. It doesn't mean a person has to be in the office of an intercessor or on a particular intercessory team. Being on a team can help a person learn more about this important subject, but it isn't necessary.

Pray passionately in the Spirit, as you constantly intercede with every form of prayer at all times. Pray the blessings of God upon all his believers.
Ephesians 6:18 TPT

The phrase "every form of prayer" lets us know that there are different types of prayer. One type of prayer that may be the most misunderstood is prophetic prayer, or prophetic intercession.

With our interest in the supernatural miracle realm comes the awareness of the significance of the ministry of prophetic intercession, along with the need for instruction.

Is there a difference between regular intercessory prayer and prophetic intercession?

Many intercessors use the term *intercession* and *prophetic intercession* interchangeably, as if they are one and the same. But are they the same type of intercession, or are they two different ways to pray?

The definition of each of these words make it clear that *prophetic intercessory prayer* and *regular intercessory prayer* are two different ways in which to pray. After the definitions, you will read examples of each type of prayer.

Prophetic intercession

Prophetic: accurately describing or predicting what will happen in the future.

The person may start out with a regular prayer of petition. Then suddenly, they feel led of the Holy Spirit to decree something. This turns the prayer into a prophetic prayer.

For a prayer to be defined as prophetic, it will contain an answer or a God given revelation within the prayer. The person making their petition to the Lord may feel led to decree a prophetic statement that prophesies how the issue they are praying about is going to be fulfilled. In the following scripture, the prophet Isaiah declares the Word of the Lord with an instruction to speak the end from the beginning.

> *Declaring the end from the beginning, and from ancient times the things that are not yet done, saying, My counsel shall stand, and I will do all my pleasure. Isaiah 46:10 NKJV*

A person may feel led by the Holy Spirit to declare a word from the Lord or perform some type of symbolic act as they pray. It's possible to receive a word or a picture in our mind of a movement to perform that comes directly from God through the Holy Spirit.

In other words, the revelation a prophetic intercessor receives from God comes "from heaven to earth." God uses the prophetic revelation released on the earth through the intercessor as an instrument to make the kingdom of heaven (the unseen spiritual realm) visible on the earth.

The intercessor's prayer or decree would be in agreement with what is on God's heart. It's a spiritual connection from heaven to earth, and the petition or declaration flows effortlessly as the Holy Spirit imparts it and the intercessor releases it.

> *For no prophecy was ever made by an act of human will, but men moved by the Holy Spirit spoke from God. 2 Peter 1:21*

Intercession: to make intercession; originally "to strike upon," or "against"; then in a good sense, "to assail anyone with petitions," "to urge," and when on behalf of another, "to intercede."

A prayer of intercession (also known as a prayer of petition) is a request made to God that asks Him to fulfill a need. Most people are motivated to come before God with a request for something they want the Lord to do for them. This would be considered a regular prayer of intercession.

Many times, a non-prophetic prayer of intercession is presented to the Lord on behalf of a person, place or thing.

This type of intercessory prayer usually originates from the mind of man.

> *Do not be anxious or worried about anything, but in everything [every circumstance and situation] by prayer and petition with thanksgiving, continue to make your [specific] requests known to God. Philippians 4:6*

We see an example in the New Testament where the church was praying fervently for the release of Peter while he was in jail. The text doesn't tell us how they were praying, but the Lord answered their prayer. The story reveals the power of agreement when we pray in unity to the Lord.

The most important thing about this scripture is to bring attention to the direct connection between our intercessory prayer and petition to God, and the mobilization of the heavenly host to act on our behalf.

> *So Peter was kept in prison, but fervent and persistent prayer for him was being made to God by the church. The very night before Herod was to bring him forward, Peter was sleeping between two soldiers, bound with two chains, and sentries were in front of the door guarding the prison.*
>
> *Suddenly, an angel of the Lord appeared [beside him] and a light shone in the cell. The angel struck Peter's side and awakened him, saying, "Get up quickly!" And the chains fell off his hands. The angel said to him, "Prepare yourself and strap on your sandals [to get ready for whatever may happen]." And he did so. Then the angel told him, "Put on your robe*

and follow me." And Peter went out following the angel. He did not realize that what was being done by the angel was real, but thought he was seeing a vision.

When they had passed the first guard and the second, they came to the iron gate that leads into the city. Of its own accord it swung open for them; and they went out and went along one street, and at once the angel left him. When Peter came to his senses, he said, "Now I know for certain that the Lord has sent His angel and has rescued me from the hand of Herod and from all that the Jewish people were expecting [to do to me]." When he realized what had happened, he went to the house of Mary the mother of John, who was also called Mark, where many [believers] were gathered together and were praying continually [and had been praying all night].
Acts 12:5-12

We can only imagine their joy when Peter appeared at the door in answer to their prayers!

Examples

Here is another example of regular intercessory prayer. It comes directly from prayer website. [1]

Prayer for prosperity and financial release:

Father, I'm here before You today because I want You to perform a miracle in my life. At this point, I cannot do it alone, and even if I could, it cannot

---

[1] www.holylandprayer.com/prayer_for/prayer-for-prosperity

be compared to Your deeds. I walk in Your sight and I can personally testify to the other miracles in my life. God, I pray for financial release in the form of employment/my business. I pray that You lift my head so that I may stand proud as one of Your children. I want You to make me a living testimony and shame the enemies who doubted Your great works in my life. I thank You, oh God my Father. In Jesus Name, Amen.

As we can see this person is not actually prophetically decreeing what the Lord says He will do for them. They are petitioning or asking Him to answer their prayer and do things for them.

Here is an example of that same prayer if it were to be a prophetic prayer of intercession.

Father, I come before You today to decree Your Word and Your will over my life. I first repent if I have any sin in my life that could be blocking my blessing in any area, especially my finances. I ask that You forgive me for all my sins and that You move me into Your grace and mercy and extend Your favor upon my life.

You say in Your Word that I will declare a thing and it shall be established for me and Your light shall shine on my path. You also say, "*For I know the plans I have for you,*" *declares the LORD, "plans to prosper you and not to harm you, plans to give you hope and a future.*

I thank You for the many ways in which You will prosper me spiritually, financially, physically, and emotionally. I am looking forward to the miracle You are going to perform for me in my life. I know that I cannot do it alone, and even if I could, it cannot be compared to Your deeds.

I thank You that You are coming to my rescue. I declare what You say in Your Word for me which is, "I will deliver him; I will protect him, because he knows My name. When he calls to Me, I will answer him; I will be with him in trouble; I will rescue him and honor him."

I thank You for sending the angels to fulfill Your Word that I am decreeing over my life. I thank You that You are answering my petition to shine Your light on my future as to my business and my employment. I will receive Your divine revelation and help concerning my future. In Jesus precious name, amen. [2]

Decreeing

The definition of *decree* is an official order issued by a legal authority. As we decree the authority of God's Word, we are actually legislating it into action. In other words, when we speak God's Word out loud, we birth it on the earth.

Legislators enforce, create and repeal laws in the natural. God's Word is known as the law. Spiritual legislators or intercessors can do what earthly legislators do. By our scriptural decrees, we are enforcing God's Word, His law—as to what He as the King, ordains to happen on earth. As we speak a decree from the scriptures, or by way of Holy

---

[2] Job 22:28, Psalm 91:15, Jerermiah 29:11

Spirit inspired speech, it is a royal decree sent forth from the throne of the King.

Testimony for Prophetic Intercession.

This is a true story about a decree over a month-old baby that reveals the power of the Word. The Word itself has the power and ability to perform and fulfill itself in a baby that has no ability to have any measure of faith. The spoken or decreed Word proved itself to be true by demonstrating its power in the physical. The mother of the baby and I only had to decree God's written Word over the baby.

Here is the story, the prayer, and the testimony.

A friend asked me to pray for her daughter's month old baby girl. From the day she was born she wouldn't sleep unless someone was holding her. The doctors couldn't find a physical cause for her distress, but if the person holding her laid her down, she would scream as if she were in extreme pain and terrible fear.

The three weeks before her birth had been an emotionally difficult and a fearful time for the mom. The baby had stopped moving and she was sure something was wrong and she felt that her baby was dying inside of her. She kept calling the clinic who handled her pregnancy, telling them her concerns. She was also worried because she wasn't gaining any weight in the last trimester as she should have been.

They checked her several times and, even though it was unusual for the baby not to move, they were able to get a heartbeat and told her nothing was wrong. This went on for three weeks. Finally, because of the mother's distress, they decided to take the baby a week early.

When the baby was born she looked as if she had been starving to death, which may have accounted for the extreme fear manifesting in this baby and not allowing her to sleep if she wasn't being held. Maybe she quit moving those last few weeks because she was using all of her energy to stay alive. The doctor told her that if they had waited to deliver the baby until she was full term, she may not have made it.

The parents and my friend, who was the grandmother, had been taking turns holding her since her birth. The baby's father had to go back to work and my friend had to go home, which was several states away. When I talked with the baby's mom over the phone, she was exhausted and crying.

I spoke with the mom for a few minutes, explaining what we were going to do, and that she would be able to participate in the prayer for her daughter. I told her that when it came to her part to pray, she could repeat the words I was speaking over her daughter. The mom is a believer, but I could do this with someone who isn't a believer also. You never know what God will use to bring a person to a saving knowledge of Jesus.

This story gives a practical everyday life example of a regular prayer of intercession with the prophetic intercession included. It is an action of rehearsing the Word of God by asking the Lord for something, reciting it as a petition, then decreeing the answer as a divine prophecy. God tells us to decree His word that was written centuries ago and bring it into the present, and He will dispatch His angels to bring the Word to fulfillment.

I am including the prayer, in case there is someone reading this who knows of a similar problem. I had prepared the scriptures that pertained to this situation in advance and paraphrased them so I could read to the baby. I have included the references for them at the end of the prayer.

> *Prophetic Intercession is an action of rehearsing the Word of God by asking the Lord for something, reciting it as a petition, then decreeing the answer as a divine prophecy.*

The mom put the phone on speaker.
We were in agreement as I read the scriptures aloud to the baby. I began by stating what God had to say about this subject in His Word. It became a declaration of blessing over her that declared the end from the beginning.

> *You will also decide and decree a thing, and it will be established for you; And the light [of God's favor] will shine upon your ways. Job 22:27-28*

I began the prayer by saying:

> Dear Heavenly Father, we thank You for hearing our prayer today on behalf of this baby. Thank You that You have been waiting for us to petition You to perform a miracle on her behalf, as a witness to Your goodness, grace and mercy, and great love. We thank You that Your Word tells us that You have a special love and concern for children, and You desire to enfold them in Your arms and bless them. In Mark 10:16, Your Word says that You took the children in Your arms,

placed Your hands on them and blessed them. We are asking You to wrap Your arms around her today and bless her with peace, as we bless her by repeating Your own words over her.

As she lay sleeping in her mother's arms, I said to her,

I am speaking spirit to spirit to you right now. My words are coming directly from the Holy Spirit, and flowing into your spirit, soul and body.

The Lord, Your Father says; "My child, do not be anxious or worried about anything, but in everything give thanks, and the peace of God which reassures your heart, that transcends all understanding, and stands guard over your heart and your mind is yours in Christ Jesus."

I then stood as an intercessor on behalf of the baby, speaking as if she was responding to what the Father had said through His Word to her.

My spirit responds by saying to You, Lord, thank You Father God, upon You have I relied and been sustained from my birth. You took me from my mother's womb and you have been my benefactor from that day. My praise is continually of You. I thank You, Lord, that You have chosen me and set me apart before I was born and called me through Your grace. You are pleased with me. You formed my innermost parts; You knit me together in my mother's womb. Praise You Father God!" I lay down and sleep; I awake, for the LORD sustains me."

Next, the mom repeated these words after me to decree her part to the Lord.

"Thank You, Lord that you say in Deuteronomy 7:13, You will love me and bless me and multiply me; You will also bless the fruit of my womb, and the fruit of my land. In Psalm 127:3, You say, children are a heritage of the Lord; and the fruit of the womb is your reward."

Next, she decreed these scriptures:

"My precious daughter, may the Lord bless you and keep you, protect, sustain, and guard you. May the Lord make His face shine upon you with favor, and be gracious to you, surrounding you with loving kindness; May the Lord lift up His face upon you with His divine approval, and give you peace, a tranquil heart and life. In Jesus name, Amen. "

That concluded our short but effective prayer of intercession.

(Scripture references: Philippians 4:6-7, Romans 15:13, Psalm 4:8, Jeremiah 29:11, Psalm 71:6, Psalm 139:13, Galatians 1:15, Numbers 6:24-27, Psalm 3:5, Proverbs 3:24)

The results were immediate! From that day forward, the baby has never had trouble going to sleep in her own bed and staying asleep. As of this printing, she is 3 years old and a very healthy, happy baby girl. This is a true testimony that the Word has the power and ability to fulfill itself, even in a baby who has no faith of her own. It will surely do the same for us.

I don't endorse taking just any scripture and quoting it and expect or presume the outcome. We can't manipulate the Lord. He is always in charge of the results, but He tells us in the Bible that when we decree His Word, we can be assured that it won't return void. He will use it for His purposes in the situation we are praying about. We agree with Him having His way in every situation.

> So will My word be which goes out of My mouth; It will not return to Me void (useless, without result), without accomplishing what I desire, and without succeeding in the matter for which I sent it.
> Isaiah 55:11

You may be thinking that you don't know the scriptures to quote as you pray. I suggest you get a prayer key for different topics and carry it with you. You can find suggested scriptures for topics on your favorite ministry website. Soon you will get familiar with the scriptures and the Holy Spirit will bring them to your remembrance as you pray.

You don't have to quote the scripture reference of the Word in your prayer, because the Lord knows where it is in the Bible. We just have to say it. When we quote the Word, we bring it to life.

When we unite both types of intercessory prayer, the prayer of petition and the prophetic decree together, we are fulfilling an end time prophecy.

In Revelation, it says both the priest and the king are needed in intercession.

We are called to be both a king and a priest unto God.

He has made us kings and priests unto God and His Father; to Him be the glory and the dominion forever and ever. Amen. Revelation 1:6 KJV

There is a difference in the two positions of intercession. Both are needed in the Kingdom of Heaven. There is the prayer of the priest who petitions God, and there is the prayer of the king who decrees the Word of God. Jesus fulfills both of these positions, and we are to follow His example and become more like Him every day.

Therefore, since we have a great high priest who has ascended into heaven, Jesus the Son of God, let us hold firmly to the faith we profess. Hebrews 4:14 NIV

As modern-day priests we petition.

The way the Old Testament priests petitioned God was to perform animal sacrifices as a substitute for sin on behalf of the people. We no longer have to offer blood sacrifices for forgiveness for sin. Jesus became the living sacrifice through His blood that He shed on the cross for our sins.

The intercessor is the priest, the Ambassador of Reconciliation, who stands between God and man, making his petition as if he were Jesus, because Jesus is within us and we represent Him on the earth. As a priest, we minister before the Lord on behalf of the people, bringing our petitions before Him in Jesus name.

Our call to that position is found in 2 Corinthians 5:20.

So we are ambassadors for Christ, as though God were making His appeal through us; we [as Christ's

representatives] plead with you on behalf of Christ
to be reconciled to God.

As kings we decree the answers

Jesus is the King of kings.

> And He hath on His vesture and on His thigh a
> name written, King Of kings, and Lord of lords.
> Revelation 19:16 KJV

We are His representatives on the earth.

> Thou hast made us unto our God kings and priests,
> and we shall reign on the earth.
> Revelation 5:10 KJV

Kings don't petition people to do their bidding. A king gives
orders, a decree, either in written or verbal form. People
respond and someone is sent forth to fulfill the wishes of
the king. *Decree:* an official order issued by a legal authority.

As intercessors, we could be missing a huge opportunity to
see our prayers and petitions answered in a greater way if
we don't prophesy God's will in the intercession. As we
release the prophetic prayer as a decree, God hears us and
then issues the orders to the heavenly angelic forces and
they respond. Their mission is to execute His will on the
earth, according to His Word, as we speak it.

> Bless the Lord, ye his angels that excel in strength,
> that do his commandments, hearkening unto the
> voice of his word.   Psalm 103:20 KJV

The angels were created and commissioned to assist in
fulfilling the Lord's will, not only for our individual lives, but
on behalf of regions, territories, and nations.

Are not all the angels ministering spirits sent out [by God] to serve (accompany, protect) those who will inherit salvation? [Of course, they are!] Hebrews 1:14

Through intercession we unite heaven and earth, and God will send forth His angelic host to assist us to fulfill His plans and purposes.

To summarize

By definition, *prophetic intercession* originates from the mind of God and contains a prophetic word or action that will have an impact on what is going to happen in the future. It is Holy Spirit and God inspired. It originates in heaven and comes to earth.

Regular intercession is a prayer which is in the form of a petition or request to God. It usually originates from the mind of man and is directed to heaven. It comes from a man or woman's soul. It is a petition asking God to do something for them. It doesn't offer any prophetic decree of what God will perform on behalf of their petition.

Every intercessor is a person who makes up the hedge, who stands between God and man on behalf of man. As we intercede on behalf of someone or something, we should move it into the prophetic by decreeing God's prophetic Word. God desires His people prophesy the answers to their prayers.

If we don't prophetically decree the Word, we are fulfilling our priestly role but neglecting our God-given kingly role.

Chapter 2

The Purpose of Prophetic Intercession

Ancient mysteries – present day significance

Remember the former things of old, for I am God, and there is no other. I am God and there is none like me, declaring the end from the beginning, and from ancient time's things that are not yet done. Saying, "My counsel shall stand, and I will do all my pleasure." Isaiah 46:9-10

The Word instructs us to remember God's former works, including the prophecies spoken or performed through the prophets. We can see that quite a number of the prophecies we read have been fulfilled. Some prophecies came to pass quickly. A number of them may have taken hundreds of years to be accomplished. This written record of history proves to all who read it that the Bible is faithful and true.

It is possible that some of the things prophesied in the Bible are to be fulfilled in our lifetime, and possibly through our actions or our words.

As we review the testimony of prophetic actions performed in the Bible, we can see the great potential there is in "performing the Word." We can gain an understanding of how the use of symbolic prophetic intercession weaves intercessors into the spiritual tapestry of every past generation. Because God lives in eternity, we have the privilege and the opportunity of spiritually partnering with the people of ancient days.

We have been given the chance to transcend time through specific actions and prayers or decrees to ensure that God's purposes come to pass. Each of our lives fit into a preordained schedule in history. Our timeline on the earth has already been written. Our time here is short from eternity's standpoint; it has an expiration date on it and so do we.

> Yet you do not know [the least thing] about what may happen in your life tomorrow. [What is secure in your life?] You are merely a vapor [like a puff of smoke or a wisp of steam from a cooking pot] that is visible for a little while and then vanishes [into thin air]. James 4:14

This is confirmed in Ecclesiastes 3:2:

> There is a time to be born and a time to die; a time to plant and a time to uproot what is planted.

The following scripture confirms that we were built right into God's program, His plan for this time in history, before we were conceived in our mother's womb, and we do have a part to play.

> My frame was not hidden from You when I was being formed in secret [and] intricate-ly and curiously wrought [as if embroidered with various colors] in the depths of the earth [a region of darkness and mystery]. Your eyes saw my unformed substance, and in Your book all the days

[of my life] were written before ever they took shape, when as yet there was none of them.
Psalm 139:15-16

It's only natural that we ask the question, "What part am I to play in God's design of this spiritual structure that He is working on in our day?" We each have a prophetically ordained part to play in order to fulfill that which has been specifically appointed to each of us. We know that God will use us to bring the revelation of His light to this dark world.

Before I formed you in the womb I knew you (and approved of you as My chosen instrument) And before you were born I consecrated you (to Myself as My own); I have appointed you as a prophet to the nations. Jeremiah 1:5

Timing of prophetic actions

If God instructs a person to perform a prophetic act, it is because He has a reason and a timing that is crucial for His desired result to happen. In order for the word the Lord gives to us to come alive we must apply it—which means to put action to it. When we do that, it springs to life as we allow it to manifest through our actions. It might come through a simple inspiration or a glimpse in the spirit. We need to pray into it.

Our actions may not always be understood, but that shouldn't keep us from following what the Holy Spirit tells us to do. If we attempt to reason out logically the thing the Lord is telling us to do, the Word says the mind is usually at enmity with God.

*Because the carnal mind is enmity against God; for
it is not subject to the law of God, neither indeed
can be.   Romans 8:7 KJV*

When you think the Holy Spirit is telling you to perform a prophetic act, it helps to discuss it with friends who move in the same prophetic flow as you do. If this is new to you, the ideal situation is to find someone who can mentor you. Maybe it will take some patient time of prayer to see the doors open for you in the area the Lord is having you target.

It can be a personal challenge to resist the urge to waste precious time questioning if the voice you are hearing is God. It is easy to listen to your own mind and human logic and argue with the voice that may be the Holy Spirit, until the feeling or thought to act passes. If this happens consistently, it's not long before the Holy Spirit doesn't use the person in this way anymore. There is a saying that could apply in this situation: "If you don't use it you lose it." God already knew how you would react so it's no surprise to Him. Don't let the enemy beat you up. Just repent, humbly ask forgiveness, and set your resolve to do better the next time.

As we follow God's directions, our prophetic actions can and will produce far reaching effects. we are His mouth, hands and feet on this earthly realm, just like the believers of old. This is our God-given spiritual inheritance. He wants us to work in partnership with Him to fulfill His will on the earth. I think we all desire to leave a legacy of testimonies that can be used by Him to instruct and equip future generations of intercessors as long as the earth remains.

In a manner of speaking, the generations that came before us are passing the baton, or the "rod of His Word," on to us.

We each possess a vital portion of the framework the Lord is building spiritually through His people, to sustain the continuing fulfillment of His farsighted prophetic vision.

All of heaven is watching to see what we will do with the segment of history that is written in His book concerning our lives. It is the will of the Lord that we search out our mission, with the help of the Holy Spirit, and walk alongside the Father for an incredible journey of exploits. This will be an exciting adventure for us if we choose to accept His mission. If we are willing, we can perform and complete our portion and help to mentor those coming along behind us. They may work with us for a time until our assignments here on earth are finished. Then we get to become a part of the great cloud of witnesses cheering others on, as we are now being cheered on by those in the stands of heaven watching us.

> Therefore, since we are surrounded by such a great cloud of witnesses, let us throw off every encumbrance and the sin that so easily entangles, and let us run with endurance the race set out for us. Hebrews 12:1

Not only are witnesses watching, but the angels are watching, eagerly assisting, and protecting us as we perform our part. The following scripture shows us yet another picture of the reality of the unseen spiritual realm.

> Then Elisha prayed and said, "Lord, please, open his eyes that he may see." And the Lord opened the servant's eyes and he saw; and behold, the mountain was full of horses and chariots of fire surrounding Elisha. 2 Kings 6:17

The Ancient Path

God tells us in Jeremiah 6:16, Stand at the crossroads and look. Ask for the ancient path and good way and walk in it.

Matthew Henry's Concise Commentary on this scripture helps us understand what the Lord is saying to us:

> Oh that men would be wise for their souls! Ask for the old paths; the way of godliness and righteousness has always been the way God has owned and blessed. Ask for the old paths set forth by the written Word of God. When you have found the good way, go on in it, you will find abundant recompense at your journey's end. But if men will not obey the voice of God and flee to His appointed Refuge, it will plainly appear at the Day of Judgment, that they are ruined because they reject God's word.

This path is the path of righteousness that those throughout the centuries have followed. On this supernatural path we will lead as exciting lives as our forefathers who walked before us. The Word describes our forefathers as:

> ...those who by [the help of] faith subdued kingdoms, administered justice, obtained promised blessings, closed the mouths of lions.
> Hebrews 11:33

Keep Asking, Seeking, Knocking

So I say to you, ask, and it will be given to you; seek, and you will find; knock, and it will be opened to you. For everyone who asks receives, and he who seeks finds, and to him who knocks it

*will be opened. If a son asks for bread from any
father among you, will he give him a stone? Or if he
asks for a fish, will he give him a serpent instead
of a fish? Or if he asks for an egg, will he offer him
a scorpion? If you then, being evil, know how to
give good gifts to your children, how much more
will your heavenly Father give the Holy Spirit to
those who ask Him!   Luke 11:9-13*

Sometimes you may think you are going in the wrong
direction because you have obstacles that pop up, but it may
be the correct way. The Lord is faithful to answer us when
we ask Him.

*Your ears will hear a word behind you, "This is the
way, walk in it," whenever you turn to the right or
to the left.   Isaiah 30:21*

Understanding the mind of the prophet

I have had many people tell me they did not understand the
subject of prophetic intercession and they have been put off
by some of the actions that people perform. They have
heard a person say that God told them to do certain things,
and said that what they were doing is called prophetic
intercession. By not understanding this type of prayer they
reject it. They think the people who call themselves
prophetic intercessors are too emotional, distracting, and
put on a show for attention. And it is possible they could be
afraid the Lord will tell *them* to do something in front of
people that they don't want to do.

What if God chooses to use someone that you don't think
you are able to receive anything from? Their personality, and

the way they present the Word that they say is from God makes you want to stay away from them.

There are times I have rejected the person and their actions when they are giving the prophecy, but I have still been able to receive the word because I felt it was from the Lord. I realized that it was just that I didn't agree with their presentation, which I know that a lot of times originates from the person's personality or how they have been taught.

There is much scriptural documentation of prophets in the Old Testament who were given prophetic utterances from God that were right on, but they were strange fellows. They might say, "Thus sayeth the Lord," or "For thus sayeth the Lord God of Israel unto me," or "Thus saith the Lord God of Hosts." This was how the prophets of old told whoever they were speaking to that their message was coming directly from God through them.

Some prophetic people today preface their prophetic words the same way, which may seem strange to us. To help us, God has set up guidelines in the Bible concerning prophecy.

1 Thessalonians 5:20-21 says:

> *Do not scorn or reject gifts of prophecy or prophecies [spoken revelations—words of instruction or exhortation or warning]. But test all things carefully [so you can recognize what is good]. Hold firmly to that which is good.*

The Word is clear that the Lord will reveal His will to His prophets.

> *Surely the Lord God will do nothing, but He revealeth His secret unto His prophets. Amos 3:7 KJV*

As a praying people, we need to commit to do as the Lord says even though we may not have a natural knowledge concerning what the Lord wants to accomplish through our prophetic actions of intercession. We need to be careful not to judge a person who we think is weird and doesn't make sense to us. God thinks differently than we do.

I am sure King David's wife, Michal, had no idea what it would cost her personally when she chose to make fun of David's dance before the Lord. Her judgment displeased God and it cost her dearly. As a result God judged her for her judgment against David and cursed her with barrenness. She was unable to bear children.

> *When David returned home to bless his own family, Michal, the daughter of Saul, came out to meet him. She said in disgust, "How distinguished the king of Israel looked today, shamelessly exposing himself to the servant girls like any vulgar person might do!"*
>
> *David retorted to Michal, "I was dancing before the LORD, who chose me above your father and all his family! He appointed me as the leader of Israel, the people of the LORD, so I celebrate before the LORD. Yes, and I am willing to look even more foolish than this, even to be humiliated in my own eyes! But those servant girls you mentioned will indeed think I am distinguished! So Michal, the daughter of Saul, remained childless throughout her entire life.   2 Samuel 6:16-23*

As children of God, our goal is to be sold out to Him. And if He tells us to do something, we need to follow through and do it. If what we say or do isn't accepted by people, then it's up to God to handle it.

I have found that many times a word of explanation helps immensely. When a person explains to those around them what they feel God is telling them to do and why, people tend to move into agreement. We don't have to be mysterious, weird and defensive about how people will react. We don't have to make a big show when we do what God is asking of us either. We are to quietly go about our business, completing our mission from God. Sometimes we can perform an action that the Lord is telling us to do right in the middle of a crowd and no one even notices.

We don't want to be deceived.

People can mean well, but a prophetic word that someone gives could be originating from their emotional self, also known as their soul, instead of from the Holy Spirit. People have to learn to hear God's voice. To hear God's voice takes practice. It's like learning to drive a car. You don't just get in the car and go out on the highway alone, you have a period of training. You have to get a license to drive without an instructor. Remember the saying, "Practice makes perfect." Those who receive prophetic words need to practice to flow in this anointing.

It doesn't cost us anything to extend grace to a person when we don't have a clear witness from the Lord to a word that someone is giving as a "thus sayeth the Lord."

We aren't required to embrace a word spoken through a prophet if we don't witness that it is from God.

Beloved, do not believe every spirit [speaking through a self-proclaimed prophet]; instead test the spirits to see whether they are from God, because many false prophets and teachers have gone out into the world. By this you know and recognize the Spirit of God: every spirit that acknowled- ges and confesses [the fact] that Jesus Christ has [actually] come in the flesh [as a man] is from God [God is its source]; and every spirit that does not confess Jesus [acknowledging that He has come in the flesh, but would deny any of the Son's true nature] is not of God; this is the spirit of the antichrist, which you have heard is coming, and is now already in the world.   1 John 4:1-3

The prophetic person can usually see when something is wrong when others don't.

In my experience, when I have been around those who operate in the office of the prophet or prophetess, they aren't usually as empathetic as the regular intercessor. They see things as either black or white. There isn't a gray area for them. They have a gift from God to sense when someone or something is not what it seems to be.

The prophetic intercessor doesn't have to be in the office of a prophet to receive a word from the Lord and perform prophetic intercession. God's choice of a prophetic inter- cessor may not be the person you would expect.

For instance, I am sure that Moses felt he would be the last person on earth that God would ask to do something for his fellow man. Moses was minding his own business, tending his sheep in the desert when God called to him out of a burning bush. God also used his brother, Aaron, because Moses asked him to. God turned Moses and Aaron into prophetic intercessors in order to warn Pharaoh that He was going to perform His will against the gods of Egypt.

> *There the angel of the Lord appeared to him in flames of fire from within a bush. Moses saw that though the bush was on fire it did not burn up. So Moses thought, "I will go over and see this strange sight—why the bush does not burn up." When the Lord saw that he had gone over to look, God called to him from within the bush, "Moses! Moses!" And Moses said, "Here I am."*
> *Exodus 3:2-4 NIV*

The angel of the Lord told Moses that he was to return to Egypt, and that He would direct him as to what he was to do there. God shared with Moses what would happen as he performed these special acts.

This is what made it prophetic intercession. God told Moses what he would do, and what the result of his prophetic actions would be. God prophesied and then fulfilled it through human intercessors.

Moses was told to use a rod (that God Himself called the "Rod of God") to perform the signs and wonders. The rod was a point of contact and symbolized God's Word being spoken to Pharaoh. The Lord used a humble intercessor who was faithful to perform and say what God said, in order to save an entire nation.

> *And by a prophet (Moses) the Lord brought Israel up from Egypt, And by a prophet Israel was preserved.* *Hosea 12:13*

We can read all the details of the prophetic intercession Moses and Aaron performed at the Lord's direction in Exodus 4:1 thru 12:1-37. Moses and Aaron were ordinary people who God used to perform supernatural exploits, all for His divine purposes.

The heavenly host assisted. It was the angel of death who passed over their dwellings on the final night, who killed all the first born in Egypt except for those who had the sign of the covenant over their doorposts.

> For the Lord will pass through to strike the Egyptians; and when He sees the blood on the lintel [above the entry way] and on the two doorposts, the Lord will pass over the door and will not allow the destroyer to come into your houses to slay you. Exodus 12:23

Some translations translate the *destroyer* as "angel of death."

Can we imagine doing some of the things God asked Moses and Aaron to do? What He asks us to do may not be as dramatic as what He told them to do, but it will be significant to Him even if it doesn't seem so important to us.

A person may be instructed by the Holy Spirit to wave a flag, banner, or other item. An instruction from God can happen anytime, but often happens during praise and worship or times of prayer. You may receive directions to do something at another location, or you may receive a directive from the Lord that is for a time in the future.

The main thing is to be willing to hear from the Lord. Ask Him to speak to you. This is not to say, of course, that the Lord can't speak to anyone on His own without them asking.

If you haven't ever heard the Lord say something to you, then ask Him.

> *Call unto me, and I will answer thee, and shew thee great and mighty things, which thou knowest not.   Jeremiah 33:3 KJV*

Another question to think about is, are you listening? People who hear from God have tuned their ears and their spirits to hear from God and they pay attention. Ask the Lord for ears to hear and eyes to see.

> *Having eyes do you not see, and having ears do you not hear? And do you not remember?*
> *Mark 8:18 ESV*

Jesus encourages us to do what His Word says.

> *We must work the works of Him who sent Me while it is day; night is coming when no one can work.*
> *John 9:4*

The more we read and know His Word, the better we will be able to think like He thinks. He isn't restricted in any area. We restrict ourselves when we look at a situation, think it is impossible, and reject the Word.

Chapter 3

Prophetic Intercession is about Relationship not Religion

I have heard some interesting viewpoints about why there is a hesitancy in some people to step out into prophetic intercession if it requires a person to rehearse or act out something the Lord tells them to do.

Most believers don't have a problem with prophetically decreeing the scriptures over a situation, but they resist rehearsing what God wants them to do in the physical that may involve some kind of action in front of people, especially if it has the potential to make them look foolish. God gives us opportunities to work out our insecurities. His thought process is different than ours.

> "For My thoughts are not your thoughts, nor are your ways My ways," says the Lord. "For as the heavens are higher than the earth, so are My ways higher than your ways, and My thoughts than your thoughts. Isaiah 55: 8-9

Most of us have a western way of thinking. We think logically, influenced by the way we have been raised and what type of Christianity, or lack of, that we are familiar with. Maybe what God is asking doesn't seem logical to us, but we can't see God's long range plan. He may ask us to fill in our piece of the eternal puzzle that completes part of His bigger plan.

I recently read an explanation about the acting out of prophetic intercession that makes perfect sense. The article I am going to quote is titled *Hebrew Thinking vs. Greek Thinking.* The following information is a small portion of the article. The article is written by Rabbi Neil Lash of Jewish Jewels in Ft. Lauderdale, Florida. He said he received his information from Dr. Randall Smith, who taught him the difference between Hebrew and Greek thinking.

> The Greek mindset focused on "What do you think?" What do you believe? We see this in Acts 17:21 where Rabbi Saul (Paul) is in Athens, the capital of Greece, and we are told, "all the Athenians and the foreigners who were there spent their time in nothing else but either to tell or hear some new thing"
>
> The Hebrews focused on relationship and action. These two aspects are mentioned over and over again in the Scriptures, both the Old and the New Testaments.
>
> First and most important is RELATIONSHIP. "I am the God of Your father—The God of Abraham, The God of Isaac, and the God of Jacob. (Exodus 3:6).
>
> The second is ACTION, which proceeds from relationship. "I am Your God who brought you out of the land of Egypt." Exodus 20:2

Action and relationship comprise the very nature of God in whose image we are made. The Scripture tells us,

So God created man in His own image; in the image of God He created him; male and female He created them. Genesis 1:27

Man was created for action.

Then the Lord God took the man and put him in the Garden of Eden to tend and keep it. Genesis 2:15.

Woman was created for relationship.

"It is not good that man should be alone; I will make him a helper comparable to him." Genesis 2:18.

The two together represent the nature of God – Action and Relationship; Hebrew thinking. Those who have a close relationship with God will want to take an active part in their connection with God so when He tells them to do something they will follow through and do it. God is our father.

Religion vs. Spirit

If a person has been living a religious lifestyle without a relationship with Jesus, it will become apparent if they get involved with a prophetic person or a prophetic group of people. The spirit of religion can't put up with a person who flows with the Holy Spirit. The Word says it will be foolishness to them. A person who is religious instead of spiritual is called a natural man.

But the natural (unbelieving) man does not accept the things [the teachings and revelations] of the Spirit of God, for they are foolishness [absurd and illogical] to him; and he is incapable of understanding them, because they are spiritually discerned and appreciated, [and he is unqualified to judge spiritual matters].   1 Corinthians 2:14

If satan can't convince a person to hate God, then he will try to turn them to religion. He will do anything to keep a person from having a personal relationship with God.

A religious person will be afraid of making God mad at them. They live by a strict set of rules because they think living life by the rules will make them righteous and earn them a pass into heaven when they die.

If a person is religious and not spiritual, they have been taken captive and need to be delivered and set free to develop their relationship with Jesus.

Religion is predictable and the Holy Spirit isn't.

When the Holy Spirit begins to move in a meeting, a religious person will get uncomfortable. Religion removes the relationship ingredient needed to build faith.

Jesus came to earth so man could have a relationship with the God who created the universe. I am not saying a religious person doesn't love the Lord, but religion is a hard taskmaster.

To be a part of the Kingdom of God, you have to walk by the spirit and have a relationship with Jesus. Jesus addresses the religious leaders in Matthew 23:13:

What sorrow awaits you teachers of religious law and you Pharisees; Hypocrites! For you shut the door of the Kingdom of Heaven in people's faces.

You won't go in yourselves, and you don't let others enter either. (NLT)

Personal relationship with God doesn't mean that we don't follow a standard that is set by rules. He gave us the Ten Commandments to live by. Religion interprets them with a different mindset than relationship does. Religion turns them into a threat, almost like a punishment.

What if we read them with a different mindset? It could be read as a command. The religious person would read it this way: *"Thou shall have no other gods before me!"*

But for a person who operates in the Holy Spirit and has a personal relationship with the Lord it would be read with this focus instead: *Because you love Me, you won't have any other gods before Me.* Our decree over this commandment would be: Because I love You, I won't even have a desire to place any foreign gods before You. I worship You and You alone are on the throne of my heart.

As believers who are born again, our relationship is truly a love relationship with God the Father, Jesus Christ the Son and the Holy Spirit. We view His commandments as a blessing to us. Our goal is to mature and develop so we don't operate out of our logical "must make sense" mindsets that many of us struggle with when it comes to the prophetic realm.

We want to get to the point where we feel free to say or perform anything our heavenly Father tells us to do. We don't want to question and reason everything until we miss our window of opportunity to bring heaven to earth. We don't want to regret what we didn't do or say because of our own self imposed limitations. The goal should be to hear and act.

We can prepare for our prophetic assignments by deliberately and purposely working to conform our minds to the fact that our lives on this earth are temporary, and that we are citizens of the Kingdom of Heaven. We have to train ourselves to look at every situation not only in a physical way, but to see it through spiritual eyes. We can expect our minds to argue with this. The disciples and believers had this same problem. It isn't a new one, but we can be overcomer's and obtain the victory.

The disciples had to fight thinking of things religously. Jesus was constantly trying to get them to look at things through the eyes of the Spirit. The Word exhorts us that we are to be spiritually minded.

> *For we walk by faith, not by sight [living our lives in a manner consistent with our confident belief in God's promises.] 2 Corinthians 5:7*

Religious leaders accused Jesus and were responsible for the terrible time He and His disciples had to endure. Saul was a religious leader and hated believers until God intervened in his life and showed him the truth. And then he spent the rest of his life instructing people how to live in relationship with Jesus and follow His commandments, out of love for the Savior. Jesus says:

> *"Come to Me, all who are weary and heavily burdened [by religious rituals that provide no peace], and I will give you rest [refreshing your souls with salvation].Take My yoke upon you and learn from Me [following Me as My disciple], for I*

am gentle and humble in heart, and you will find rest (renewal, blessed quiet) for your souls. For My yoke is easy [to bear] and My burden is light." Matthew 11:28-30

As we continue to walk in the Spirit it will become more natural for us. There are spiritual principals that we develop as we mature. One of them is to realize the importance of reading the Word daily. As we read the Bible, it has the power to cleanse us of old belief systems and feed our spirit man. We may not realize it at the time, but as we read the Word it does the work necessary within us. The Word says it will cleanse and wash away old mindsets and attitudes as we walk on the path the Lord has ordained for us.

So that He might sanctify the church, having cleansed her by the washing of water with the word [of God]. Ephesians 5:26

The Word of God is powerful enough to deliver us as it promises.

As we receive the Word of God and allow it to absorb into our minds and spirits, it is powerful enough to cut right through barriers our soul nature has built up. Our soul nature is our willful, emotional nature. The Word will be received by our spirit man as food so we can grow into maturity in Christ.

For the word of God is quick, and powerful, and sharper than any two-edged sword, piercing even to the dividing asunder of soul and spirit, and of the joints and marrow, and is a discerner of the thoughts and intents of the heart. Hebrews 4:12 NKJV

Our struggle will end as we realize that what we feed will grow and what we starve will die. If we feed our spirit man on the food of the Word, he will grow. If we feed ourselves with the food of the world and its temptations, we will grow away from spiritual godly things.

As we exert self discipline against the temptations and addictions of the world, and chase after God by reading His Word, we begin to get the revelation of how important it is to cultivate an atmosphere of praise to Him in our everyday lives. This daily pattern will cause us to be successfully set free from all captivity and ungodly entanglements, and we will receive the promised blessings. Before we know it, our desire for worldly things will no longer have any power over us, and we will be set free from the fear of man that keeps us from embracing prophetic intercession.

> However, you are not [living] in the flesh [controlled by the sinful nature] but in the Spirit, if in fact the Spirit of God lives in you [directing and guiding you]. But if anyone does not have the Spirit of Christ, he does not belong to Him [and is not a child of God]. Romans 8:9

If you are reading this and it ministers personally to you because you have been raised in a religious setting, or your church is religious without promoting a relationship with Jesus, you can overcome this through humbling yourself. Repent for the sin of looking at everything through the eyes of religion, and ask for forgiveness. Tell Jesus that you want a relationship with Him. He will respond.

Religion, in itself, is dead and has no spiritual power to convert anyone. It is lacking love. The Lord warns about this type of relationship and encourages us to leave that old mindset and come into new life in the Spirit that empowers us to demonstrate His love.

> But you will receive power when the Holy Spirit has come upon you, and you will be my witnesses in Jerusalem and in all Judea and Samaria, and to the end of the earth. Acts 1:8 NIV

I am including two prayers here for the person who may be captured by this spirit of religion, or married to a person who is religious, or has relatives or friends who don't approve of the prophetic.

The first prayer is a personal prayer for yourself.

> Dear Heavenly Father, I come humbly before You to repent on behalf of any sin I have committed against You or against Your Word. I repent for the sin of being religious and ask forgiveness for the times I have spoken against others and judged them because of my religious mindset. I may have been ignorantly judging You, especially if You are the one who told the person to do something that I judged wrongly. As I ask You to forgive me for my sins, I ask that You wash away my sin by the blood of Jesus. I ask that You move any case the enemy might have against me from the Courtroom of Judgment to the Throne of Grace and Mercy and remove any veils or scales that have been over the eyes of my understanding so I will see Your truth and embrace Your truth and walk in Your truth. In Jesus name, Amen.

Intercessory prayer for others (Insert the name of the one you are praying for.)

Dear Heavenly Father I come before You humbly. I have repented of my sins and asked forgiveness. I stand before You now on behalf of _____. I bring them into Your Courtroom in Heaven. I stand in the gap as an Ambassador of Reconciliation on their behalf. I am presenting an appeal to You. I know that _____ doesn't understand my relationship with You, which is a personal relationship not a relationship of man's religion. I ask that You would forgive them if they have spoken against my personal relationship with You or judged me in any way. I forgive them as You forgive them. I ask that You will move on their life in such a way that they will have a personal loving relationship with You, Lord. I decree that You will remove any veils or scales that have been over their eyes, just like the veils or scales that were on Saul/Paul's eyes in Acts 9:18: *Immediately something like scales fell from Saul's eyes, and he regained his sight. Then he got up and was baptized.* He became a new creation in You. I thank You that_____ will see the truth and the truth will set them free. In Jesus name, Amen.

Chapter 4

Ways to Receive the Prophetic Word of the Lord

The two primary ways a person receives a word from God are through a *logos* word or a *rhema* word.

The more commonly known of these two Greek words is *logos*. A logos word is used to refer to the written Word of God. By reading the written Word we can learn about God and study His ways. We can also find prophecies that have been fulfilled and those that haven't been fulfilled yet, prophecies that could be scheduled to be fulfilled in our day.

There were times when people performed an act of prophetic intercession by reminding the Lord of the "logos" word that had been written in the scroll of the Torah and the prophets. Prophetic intercession is revealing God's plans to His people. It might be through the Word being quoted, or by actions that are in the scripture being rehearsed.

Example of a Logos Word

An example of a *logos word* is found in the book of Daniel starting at Chapter 9. As Daniel read the prophetic words spoken by the prophet Jeremiah written in a scroll, he was able to calculate the time for the prophecy to be fulfilled. He saw, by counting years that were in the prophecy, that it was to be fulfilled exactly during the time he was reading the scroll. So Daniel set himself to prayer and fasting. Here are some of the words he read.

*This whole land shall become a ruin and a waste,
and these nations shall serve the king of Babylon
seventy years. Then after seventy years are
completed, I will punish the king of Babylon and
that nation, the land of the Chaldeans, for their
iniquity, says the Lord, making the land an
everlasting waste. Jeremiah 25:11-12 ESV*

It was true, in a direct sense, that the conquest of Babylon
was a blessing for God's people. They had no release from
exile under the Babylonians, but under the Persians, the
Jews were allowed to return to the Promised Land. [3]

As Daniel stood in the gap as an Ambassador of
Reconciliation, to repent on behalf of the sins of the people
and asked God to forgive their sins, he reminded the Lord
of His mighty acts on behalf of His people in times past.

God heard his prayer and sent the angel Gabriel to bring an
answer to Daniel.

*While I was still speaking and praying, and confessing
my sin and the sin of my people Israel, and presenting
my supplication before the Lord my God in behalf of the
holy mountain of my God, while I was still speaking in
prayer and extremely exhausted, the man Gabriel,
whom I had seen in the earlier vision, came to me
about the time of the evening sacrifice. He instructed
me and he talked with me and said, "O Daniel, I have
now come to give you insight and wisdom and
understanding. At the beginning of your supplications,
the command [to give you an answer] was issued, and*

---

[3] https://enduringword.com/bible-commentary/jeremiah-51/

*I have come to tell you, for you are highly re-
garded and greatly beloved. Therefore consider the
message and begin to understand the [meaning of the]
vision." Daniel 9:21-23*

The angel Gabriel assures Daniel that God is about to act
because of the prayer of intercession that he has made to
the Lord. Gabriel told Daniel that he also required the help
of the angel Michael, because there were spiritual forces
preventing him from bringing Daniel his answer. For us, in
practical terms, that could mean what appears to be delay
is not denial of our prayers and petitions. There could be
some warfare the angelic host is engaging in on our behalf.

The Lord tells us in His Word He is watching over His Word.
It will be performed and He may use us to act out or
prophesy what he is about to perform.

*I am [actively] watching over My word to fulfill it.
Jeremiah 1:12*

Just as God dispatched an angel to Daniel, he dispatches
angels in answer to our prayers too.

*Are not all the angels ministering spirits sent out
[by God] to serve (accompany, protect) those who
will inherit salvation? [Of course they are!]
Hebrews 1:14*

Our prayers and prophetic actions can encourage the
process of fulfillment of scriptures in our day. This scripture
says that there is a veil that had been cast over the eyes of
the Hebrew children from ancient days.

*But [in fact] their minds were hardened [for they
had lost the ability to understand]; for until this*

very day at the reading of the old covenant the same veil remains unlifted, because it is removed [only] in Christ. But to this day whenever Moses is read, a veil [of blindness] lies over their heart; but whenever a person turns [in repentance and faith] to the Lord, the veil is taken away.
2 Corinthians 3:14-16

This is a logos word, much like the one that Daniel found in the writings when he began to entreat the Lord. Even though this scripture concerns the Jewish people, as intercessors we can pray into this scripture and utilize it for anyone who has a veil over their eyes and can't understand or see the truth.

As intercessors, we become Ambassadors of Reconciliation on their behalf, the veils will be removed from their eyes and they will see the truth repent, ask forgiveness for their sins and receive Jesus as their Savior. In the case of the Jewish people that God is speaking of in the scripture, when the veil comes off they change their mind (repent) and acknowledge their Messiah Yeshua has already come.

This prophetic word is given with only one stipulation and brings with it a big promise: *"But whenever a person turns [in repentance and faith] to the Lord, the veil is taken away."* The Lord promises if a person repents, asks forgiveness and turns to Him, He will remove the veil that is over the eyes of their understanding in the spiritual realm, which affects their lives in the physical realm.

We can use this scripture in a prophetic intercessory prayer along with some specific symbolic actions. We can be assured by scripture that we are praying in agreement with the will of the Lord.

> *The Lord is not slow to fulfill His promise as some understand slowness, but is patient with you, not wanting anyone to perish, but everyone to come to repentance.   2 Peter 3:9 ESV*

We can present their case in the Courtroom of Heaven through prayer and petition, standing in the gap as Ambassadors of Reconciliation. This could be considered a

---

To *pray into* simply means to pray what you see or hear. If it is a good thing, decree what God wants to accomplish as seen in the dream or vision, or heard in the prophetic word. If it is a warning that brings fear, then decree or prophecy God's will such as His protection and direction as found in Psalms 91 and Jeremiah 29:11 by personalzing the scripture.

No weapon that is formed against me will succeed; and every tongue that rises against me in judgment I will condemn. This [peace, righteousness, security, and triumph over opposition] is the heritage of the servants of the Lord, and this is their vindication from Me," says the Lord.   Isaiah 54:17

---

class action suit. That's where one person presents the case on behalf of a larger group, just as Daniel did.

Like Daniel, the Lord may bring a revelation to us, as the Ambassador of Reconciliation intercessor, to stand in the gap. As an Ambassador of Reconciliation, that believer can represent a whole nation of people as easily as they can represent one person.

If you are interested in acting out this particular scripture as a memorial to the Lord and His Word, to bring the Word to life, it is an easy thing to do. It can be done in the privacy of your home, but it has the potential of changing the lives of millions of people in many nations. Father God is watching what we are doing and He is hearing what we are saying. He will dispatch His host of angels to go forth and perform His Word on behalf of those whose hearts are prepared to receive Him. Then, as we act out the Word of God, He will remove the veils from the eyes of their understanding. This is called *symbolic prophetic intercession.*

Acting out the scripture

It's a joy to act out this scripture as a remembrance to the Lord. This is how it can be done.

Take a piece of fabric large enough to represent a veil over the eyes of the people. Hold it by two of the corners. Hold it over your head so it covers your eyes, then lift it up and symbolically act out the removing of the veil over the eyes of their understanding. I usually also act out a person lifting their hands in surrender along with this movement. Then you can place the veil over your head and decree that they are coming under the wings of the Lord, which is acting out Psalm 91.

I fully explain this symbolic acting out of the scriptures with the veil in a more detailed way in the book *Heavenly Impact—Symbolic Praise, Worship and Intercession. On Earth As It Is In Heaven.* A "symbolic movement vocabulary" is included that is based on scriptures.

As you stand in the gap, repenting on behalf of sin that is being committed against God by those who have self-imposed veils over the eyes of their understanding because of the hardness of their hearts, ask God to forgive their sin against Him. As you lift your hands in surrender on their behalf, you are symbolizing their asking forgiveness and surrendering to Him. He says in His Word that if we will ask Him, He will forgive us. We understand that this prophetic action will move those we are interceding for, from judgment for rejecting God, into His grace and mercy, where they will have an opportunity to repent for their own decisions. They will still have their day in court before the Judge, but the intercessor secures through Jesus, a stay of execution in the legal court system in the Heavenly Court.

We aren't asking God to forgive the person; they will have to ask for themselves. But we can intercede on behalf of the sin they are committing against God, just as Daniel did. By doing that, we can appeal to God to move any case the accuser has against them from the Courtroom of Judgment to the Throne of Grace and Mercy, and to remove the veils from the eyes of their understanding. What they do with the truth is up to them, but we will decree that they will repent before God.

God knows exactly who the person or people are that we are interceding for, and where they are spiritually. He desires to remove the veils from their eyes. As we stand in the gap repenting for their sin and asking forgiveness, we act out the removing of the veil from the eyes of their understanding. We can remind Him of the time that He did this for Saul (Paul). Religion had Saul bound, and God removed the scales/veils from his eyes and he saw the truth and the truth set him free.

According to scripture, Saul was a religious scholar—a rabbi, a teacher of teachers, but he had scales/veils over the eyes of his understanding and did not know it.

The Conversion of Saul

Now Saul, still breathing threats and murder against the disciples of the Lord [and relentless in his search for believers], went to the high priest, and he asked for letters [of authority] from him to the synagogues at Damascus, so that if he found any men or women there belonging to the Way [believers, followers of Jesus the Messiah], men and women alike, he could arrest them and bring them bound [with chains] to Jerusalem.

As he traveled he approached Damascus, and suddenly a light from heaven flashed around him [displaying the glory and majesty of Christ]; and he fell to the ground and heard a voice [from heaven] saying to him, "Saul, Saul, why are you per-secuting and oppressing Me?" And Saul said, "Who are You, Lord?" And He answered, "I am Jesus whom you are persecuting, now get up and go into the city, and you will be told what you must do." The men who were traveling with him [were terrified and] stood speechless, hearing the voice but seeing no one. Saul got up from the ground, but though his eyes were open, he could see nothing; so they led him by the hand and brought him into Damascus. And he was unable to see for three days, and he neither ate nor drank.

Now in Damascus there was a disciple named Ananias; and the Lord said to him in a vision, "Ananias." And he answered, "Here I am,

Lord." And the Lord said to him, "Get up and go to the street called Straight, and ask at the house of Judas for a man from Tarsus named Saul; for he is praying [there], and in a vision he has seen a man named Ananias come in and place his hands on him, so that he may regain his sight." But Ananias answered, "Lord, I have heard from many people about this man, especially how much suffering and evil he has brought on Your saints (God's people) at Jerusalem; and here [in Damascus] he has authority from the high priests to put in chains all who call on Your name [confessing You as Savior]." But the Lord said to him, "Go, for this man is a [deliberately] chosen instrument of Mine, to bear My name before the Gentiles and kings and the sons of Israel; for I will make clear to him how much he must suffer and endure for My name's sake."

So Ananias left and entered the house, and he laid his hands on Saul and said, "Brother Saul, the Lord Jesus, who appeared to you on the road as you came [to Damascus], has sent me so that you may regain your sight and be filled with the Holy Spirit [in order to proclaim Christ to both Jews and Gentiles]." Immediately something like scales fell from Saul's eyes, and he regained his sight. Then he got up and was baptized; and he took some food and was strengthened. Acts 9:1-19

Another area the accuser can legally get a veil placed over the eyes of a believer is if they hate or judge a fellow believer. It gives the enemy a legal right to blind the believer's eyes who hates or judges another person. They may believe they have every right to hate another or be bitter towards another, but this puts them in a position of the Judge and the enemy can blind them to the truth.

> *But anyone who hates a fellow believer is still living and walking in darkness. Such a person does not know the way to go, having been blinded by the darkness.*   *1 John 2:11 NLT*

If you know a fellow believer who has a hatred for another believer, this removing of the veil is an active symbolic form of intercession you can perform on their behalf as you decree Jeremiah 24:7:

> *I will give them a heart to know Me, [understanding fully] that I am the Lord; and they will be My people, and I will be their God, for they will return to Me with their whole heart.*

The prophetic logos Word says the Lord will visit them and give them a heart to know Him. We are acting out and decreeing "on earth as it is in heaven," which is what the Lord told us to do in the prayer that He taught the disciples to pray daily. In heaven the veils are removed, then they are removed on the earth and we can see the truth clearly.

> *Pray, then, in this way: "Our Father, who is in heaven, Hallowed be Your name. Your kingdom come, Your will be done On earth as it is in heaven." "Give us this day our daily bread. And forgive us our debts, as we have forgiven our debtors [letting go of both the wrong and the resentment]. And do not lead us into temptation, but deliver us from evil. For Yours is the kingdom*

and the power and the glory forever. Amen.
Matthew 6:9-13.

A Rhema Word

As we read stories of prophetic intercession that are demonstrated in the Bible, we see that the majority of this type of intercession was initiated by a *rhema* word from God. The meaning of the word *rhema* is a word that comes through divine inspiration by the Holy Spirit. Another way to put it is God is communicating a personal word to a person.

Rhema: Rhema (ῥῆμα in Greek) literally means an "utterance" or "thing said." It is a word that signifies the action of an utterance. [4]

Sometimes a person hears an audible voice speak a prophetic word to them. It is a word that comes from the Holy Spirit within them. The Word is coming from Jesus and the Father to bring the message from the Throne in heaven to earth. The Holy Spirit, who is a member of the Godhead, lives within us on the earth.

An angel appeared to John in Revelation 19:10:

> *Then I fell down at his feet to worship him, but he [stopped me and] said to me, "You must not do that; I am a fellow servant with you and your brothers and sisters who have and hold the testimony of Jesus. Worship God [alone]. For the testimony of Jesus is the spirit of prophecy [His life and teaching are the heart of prophecy]."*

---

[4] https://en.wikipedia.org/wiki/rhema

The Holy Spirit testifies to us what is the will of the Father; then He guides us in the way we should go to accomplish the prophetic will of God.

> But when He, the Spirit of Truth (the Truth-giving Spirit) comes, He will guide you into all the Truth (the whole, full Truth). For He will not speak His own message [on His own authority]; but He will tell whatever He hears [from the Father; He will give the message that has been given to Him], and He will announce and declare to you the things that are to come [that will happen in the future].
> John 16:13

The Spirit of Prophecy in Prophetic Intercession

We understand from the Word of God that the active person of the Godhead on the earth is the Holy Spirit. Jesus sent Him to comfort and encourage us and to bring all things to remembrance. He is the Spirit of Prophecy on the earth.

> And I will ask the Father, and He will give you another Helper (Comforter, Advocate, Intercessor—Counselor, Strengthener, Standby), to be with you forever..."
> John 14:16

While at a conference, a woman was sharing a story with me that opened my eyes to a function of the Holy Spirit that I hadn't seen before.

She told me that she was watching an evangelist on Youtube, who was well known and very active in gathering young people to large conferences in Washington DC and other locations around the United States. Their purpose was to humble themselves before God and repent and ask forgiveness for sins, not only for themselves, but for our country and government. They petition God to heal our land.

As we can imagine, there were a lot of issues with organizing this type of event. He shared that he had been complaining to the Lord about the neverending logistics required to get the vision to become the reality.

He shared that one day, out of frustration, he told the Lord that he didn't know why the Lord had called him to this. He said to the Lord, "I never asked for this government involvement on such a large scale." He shared that the Lord had quickly answered him and said; "Oh yes you did." So he asked the Lord, "When was that?" The Lord said to him, "As you have been praying in tongues the last several months, you have been prophesying over yourself My perfect will for you, and this is it."

It never occurred to me that as I pray in tongues, part of the prayer is prophesying my future—God's will for me over my life. The Holy Spirit knows exactly what I am to be about and He will lead me right into where I should be and what I should be doing.

Examples of hearing a rhema word from the Lord.

Another form of Kingdom of God language is to speak in unknown tongues. For those of us who speak in tongues, we know it is another way of communicating a word directly from the Throne of God in heaven into this realm on earth.

Because this language is a spiritual language, Jesus said a person must be what is called "born of the Spirit" to have the faith to accept and pursue the works of the Holy Spirit.

Our goal as believers is to become dependent on the Holy Spirit to lead and direct us daily.

God is a Spirit (a spiritual Being) and those who worship Him must worship Him in spirit and in truth (reality). John 4:24

Jesus answered him, "I assure you and most solemnly say to you, unless a person is born again [reborn from above—spiritually transformed, renewed, sanctified], he cannot [ever] see and experience the kingdom of God." John 3:3

To be able to participate in the ministry of symbolic prophetic intercession, it is vital that a person believes that the Holy Spirit will lead them to rehearse prophetic acts. I know believers who are born again but don't manifest the gift of speaking in tongues. They hear from the Lord and perform prophetic acts as the Holy Spirit directs them. They have been born of the Spirit.

That which is born of the flesh is flesh [the physical is merely physical], and that which is born of the Spirit is spirit. John 3:6

For you have been born again [that is, reborn from above—spiritually transformed, renewed, and set apart for His purpose] not of seed which is perishable but [from that which is] imperishable and immortal, that is, through the living and everlasting word of God. 1 Peter 1:23

A person who has the Holy Spirit activated within them can expect to hear from Him.

56

And these signs will accompany those who believe: in my name they will cast out demons; they will speak in new tongues. Mark 16:17 NIV

How are we filled with the Spirit?

The Holy Spirit entered you when you decided to give your life to Christ. Many of us don't really think about activating the Holy Spirit that came with our new life in Jesus. If you haven't asked the Holy Spirit to come alive and active in your life, and you would like to, you can pray this prayer and invite Him to play a more active part in your life.

Dear Jesus,
I thank You that, as the Son of God, You paid the price for my sins on the cross. I repent for any sins I have committed against You or Your Word. I ask that You forgive my sins, and wash them away with Your cleansing blood. I ask that You would baptize me with Your Holy Spirit, filling me up to overflowing. I give You permission to use my tongue and ask that this baptism include the manifestation of speaking in other tongues. I welcome the ministry of the Holy Spirit into my life. I thank You that You say in your Word that He, (the Holy Spirit) will comfort and encourage me. He will guide me into all truth, and He will be with me forever. Amen

Prophetic prayer is disclosing what is to come. When a Word is about something that will occur in the future, we may not have an understanding of what or when it is going to happen, but we need to decree or act out symbolically what the Lord plans to come to pass. We are led of the Spirit, even if we don't have a complete understanding of what is to come.

> But when He, the Spirit of Truth, comes, He will guide you into all the truth [full and complete truth]. For He will not speak on His own initiative, but He will speak whatever He hears [from the Father—the message regarding the Son], and He will disclose to you what is to come [in the future].
> John 16:13

It is a comfort to know that the Holy Spirit will tell us what to do and what not to do. The Holy Spirit might give us a warning or an absolute 'no' to something we are planning on doing. He may send a heavenly messenger to us in a vision or a dream. Consider the story about Paul attempting to go to Macedonia.

> Now when they had gone throughout Phrygia and the region of Galatia, and were forbidden of the Holy Ghost to preach the word in Asia, after they were come to Mysia, they assayed to go into Bithynia: but the Spirit suffered them not. And they passing by Mysia came down to Troas. And a vision appeared to Paul in the night; There stood a man of Macedonia, and prayed him, saying, Come over into Macedonia, and help us. And after he had seen the vision, immediately we endeavored to go into Macedonia, assuredly gathering that the Lord had called us to preach the gospel unto them.
> Acts 16:6-10 NKJV

This is something that happens to us, too. When we decide we are going to do something or go somewhere and it seems that it gets blocked, sometimes it is the Holy Spirit saying 'not yet.' Don't get frustrated, get glad! God will make the way at the right time. This scripture does say they were *forbidden* by the Holy Ghost, so it implies that they were seeking God in their directions. That's what we have to do concerning everything as we are led of the Spirit.

We see another example of this in the New Testament of an action of symbolic prophetic intercession that includes a warning to Paul.

> *And as we tarried there many days, there came down from Judaea a certain prophet, named Agabus. And when he was come unto us, he took Paul's girdle, and bound his own hands and feet, and said, Thus saith the Holy Ghost, So shall the Jews at Jerusalem bind the man that owneth this girdle, and shall deliver him into the hands of the Gentiles.*
>
> *Now when we heard these things, both we and those from that place pleaded with him not to go up to Jerusalem. Then Paul answered, "What do you mean by weeping and breaking my heart? For I am ready, not only to be bound, but also to die at Jerusalem for the name of the Lord Jesus. Acts 21:10-13 KJV*

Verse 14 tells how they settled it within themselves, and how they would intercede for him from that point. So *when he would not be persuaded, we ceased, saying, "The will of the Lord be done."* They didn't doubt that the prophetic word was from God, but they made the decision to leave what would happen to Paul in God's hands. That doesn't mean they didn't continue in intercession, but they changed the way they were interceding. They came into agreement with God's will.

They could have said; "Well, he won't listen to us—so whatever happens to him happens." In reading the way they prayed, we see that they were still prophetically making a decree, "The will of the Lord be done." They were keeping their opinion out of it. They didn't have the whole picture. Paul needed to go to Jerusalem, be bound and put in jail to bring forth God's purposes. Paul had the discernment to know that the word wasn't to change his mind about going, but to confirm and prepare him.

> And see, now I go bound in the spirit to Jerusalem, not knowing the things that will happen to me there, except that the Holy Spirit testifies in every city, saying that chains and tribulations await me. But none of these things move me; nor do I count my life dear to myself, so that I may finish my race with joy, and the ministry which I received from the Lord Jesus, to testify to the gospel of the grace of God.   Acts 20:22-24 NKJV

According to this scripture, the physical binding was twofold. Paul says he was bound in the Spirit, so he knew he had to go. What the prophet prophetically acted out was a picture of what would happen to him.

His visit to Jerusalem, and what would happen to him during that visit, wasn't given any credit as an attack of the enemy. Having God's perspective and hearing from Him in every situation is vital for intercessors.

If Paul didn't have the discernment that this was the will of God for his life, he might have mistakenly led the disciples in a prayer more focused toward what the enemy had planned for him. Before you know it, they might have been binding and rebuking the enemy. They would be praying incorrectly and would be off track. When the answer isn't obvious, part of maturity is discerning the answer to the question, "Is this You Lord, or is this the enemy?"

We see that Jesus was led into the wilderness for a time of testing. It was God's will, and he knew that he was being led of the Spirit and he had the victory over the devil. We, too, can have the victory during the trials and testing in our own lives.

> *Then Jesus was led by the [Holy] Spirit into the wilderness to be tempted by the devil.*
> *Matthew 4:1*

Some people see what the Lord is saying.

> *Formerly in Israel, when a man went to inquire of God, he would say, "Come, let us go to the seer," for he who is called a prophet today was formerly called a seer. 1 Samuel 9:9 NIV*

If we could see into the spiritual realm, we would be able to see the angelic army waiting to hear our decree and be released by the Lord to act on our behalf. The heavenly host is waiting in the unseen realm to perform on our behalf. In faith we believe that truth. Elisha believed and was able to see into the spiritual realm.

The Prophet Elisha was a seer.

Then Elisha prayed and said, "Lord, please, open his eyes that he may see." And the Lord opened the servant's eyes and he saw; and behold, the mountain was full of horses and chariots of fire surrounding Elisha. When the Arameans came down to him, Elisha prayed to the Lord and said, "Please strike this people (nation) with blindness." And God struck them with blindness, in accordance with Elisha's request. Then Elisha said to the Arameans, "This is not the way, nor is this the city. Follow me and I will lead you to the man whom you are seeking." And he led them to Samaria.
2 Kings 6:17-19

The seer receives a message through a type of picture, which they then release. Generally, these pictures are either received while awake by means of visions, or while asleep through dreams. You don't have to be in the office of a prophet to be able to see in the spiritual realm. God has supernaturally opened the eyes of many people today to be able to see into the spiritual realm. We even hear of unbelievers that God has revealed Himself to in a dream, vision, or word spoken, and they become believers.

Chapter 5

The Lord Speaks the Language of Symbolism

Our God is the God of symbolism. This language is often a soundless language but is heard loud and clear across the expanse of the heavens, reaching to the Throne of the Creator of the universe. This language transcends time and isn't limited in the ways it has been used throughout history. (*Heavenly Impact,* Jeanette Strauss)

God is interacting with His people today in the same way He did throughout the Old and New Testament. We are seeing a restoration of prophetic acts being performed by believers as never before.

We know from the previous chapters that Jesus loves and endorses the prophetic ministry because the Bible says He is the Spirit of Prophecy. He and the Holy Spirit are one and the same. So when the Holy Spirit reveals something prophetic from the Lord, it is coming from the Throne in Heaven.

Speaking in parables

Another aspect of symbolic, prophetic language is speaking in parables. When Jesus shared with those who had gathered to listen to Him, He communicated through parables.

Jesus spoke all these things to the crowds in parables. He did not tell them anything without using a parable. So was fulfilled what was spoken through the prophet: "I will open my mouth in parables; I will utter things hidden since the foundation of the world."   Matthew 13:34-35 NIV

A parable is a way of speaking or demonstrating something. In symbolic language, it is one thing used to represent another. They are illustrations or comparisons put beside truths to explain or demonstrate them.

I have also spoken to [you through] the prophets, And I gave [them] many visions [to make My will known]. And through the prophets I gave parables [to appeal to your sense of right and wrong]. Hosea 12:10

In today's language, Jesus would explain His use of parables in this way: "I am going to give you an object lesson using visual aids." It is easier for people to remember things by connecting them to something that they are familiar with. That's why we do object lessons in Sunday School. That is what Jesus did. He used examples from their everyday lives.

Because we aren't from Jesus' era we might not understand the parable, but we have commentaries from historians that can explain what He meant when He spoke in parables.

Speaking with symbols.

Parables are also called metaphors. Examples of speaking in a metaphor would be to say, "that person has a heart of stone," to signify they are unemotional. A "skeleton in a closet" would mean hiding a past action that is not good. "Raining cats and dogs" means it's raining very hard. We can see how these sayings wouldn't have been understood in ancient days unless someone gave the person the interpretation.

The story that follows is an example of a parable that Jesus shared with the people. They would have understood what He was talking about, but when we read the story we wouldn't identify with the object He is using to get His point across.

> Jesus said to His disciples, "I assure you and most solemnly say to you, it is difficult for a rich man [who clings to possessions and status as security] to enter the kingdom of heaven. Again I tell you, it is easier for a camel to go through the eye of a needle, than for a rich man [who places his faith in wealth and status] to enter the kingdom of God." Matthew 19:23-24

What does the symbolic language used in this parable mean? Some theorize that the needle Jesus was speaking of was the Needle Gate, supposedly a low and narrow after-hours entrance found in the wall surrounding Jerusalem. It was purposely small for security reasons, and a camel could only go through it by stripping off any saddles or packs and crawling through on its knees.

The message in the parable is that the love of money and possessions can take our eyes off of the kingdom of God, and draw us away into worldly pleasures. He is not saying that a believer can't be prosperous, but the scripture is clear that it is the love of money that is the root of all evil. He is warning that a man who is prosperous might not be willing to lay everything down to go through the narrow gate to get into the Kingdom of God.

It is interesting that the picture most of us would get when we read that parable is of a person trying to get through the eye of an actual needle, but that would be impossible and we know that to get into the Kingdom of God is possible.

Many times throughout the Bible, God instructed an intercessor or prophet to perform a symbolic prophetic act to demonstrate a prophecy that would happen in the future.

The following story found in 2 Kings 13:15-19,25, is a example of the prophet Elijah speaking a prophetic word, with an instruction to the King of Israel to rehearse a prophetic action. The symbolic prophetic act the King performed carried with it the power and authority to win a victory over the enemies of Israel.

> And Elisha said to him, "Take a bow and arrows." So he took a bow and arrows. Then he said to the king of Israel, "Put your hand on the bow." And he put his hand on it, and Elisha put his hands on the king's hands. And he said, "Open the window to the east," and he opened it. Then Elisha said, "Shoot!" And he shot. And Elisha said, "The Lord's arrow of victory, the arrow of victory over Aram (Syria); for you will strike the Arameans in Aphek until you have destroyed them." Then he said, "Take the arrows," and he took them.
>
> And Elisha said to the king of Israel, "Strike the ground," and he struck it three times and stopped. So the man of God was angry with him and said, "You should have struck five or six times; then you would have struck down Aram until you had

destroyed it. But now you shall strike Aram only three times."

In verse 25, we get to see the fulfillment of the symbolic prophetic act:

Then Jehoash (Joash) the son of Jehoahaz recovered from Ben-hadad the son of Hazael the cities which he had taken from Jehoahaz his father by war. Three times Joash defeated Ben-hadad and recovered the cities of Israel.

Another example would be when God gave the prophet Jeremiah a prophetic message that included a symbolic prophetic act or gesture.

Thus says the Lord of hosts, "The broad wall of Babylon will be completely overthrown and the foundations razed and her high gates will be set on fire; the peoples will labor in vain, and the nations become exhausted [only] for fire [that will destroy their work]."

So Jeremiah wrote in a single scroll all the disaster which would come on Babylon, [that is] all these words which have been written concerning Babylon. Then Jeremiah said to Seraiah, "When you come to Babylon, see to it that you read all these words aloud, and say, "You, O Lord, have promised concerning this place to cut it off and destroy it, so that there shall be nothing living in it, neither man nor animal, but it will be perpetually desolate." And as soon as you finish reading this scroll, you shall tie a stone to it and throw it into the middle of the Euphrates. Then say,

*'In the same way Babylon will sink down and not
rise because of the disaster that I will bring on her;
and the Babylonians will become [hopelessly]
exhausted." Thus the words of Jeremiah are
completed. Jeremiah 51:58,60-64*

Jeremiah instructed Seraiah to speak a prophetic decree:

*See to it that you read all these words aloud, and
say, "You, O Lord, have promised concerning this
place to cut it off and destroy it, so that there shall
be nothing living in it, neither man nor animal, but
it will be perpetually desolate. (verse 61-62)*

As Seraiah repeated the words as instructed by Jeremiah,
he was recounting or rehearsing the Word of the Lord back
to Him. God is always faithful to perform His own Word.
Then Seraiah performed the symbolic prophetic act to
signify what Jeremiah had instructed him to do. This
symbolic prophetic act demonstrated God's impending
judgment against Babylon.

*And as soon as you finish reading this scroll, you
shall tie a stone to it and throw it into the middle
of the Euphrates. Then say, 'In the same way
Babylon will sink down and not rise because of the
disaster that I will bring on her; and the
Babylonians will become [hopelessly] exhausted.
(verse 60-64)*

We, like Jeremiah, should record what the Lord tells us. It
says he recorded the Word of the Lord on the scroll. The
Bible instructs us to do the same thing. The runner could be
a spiritual runner, such as an angel.

*And the LORD answered me, and said, Write the
vision, and make it plain upon tables, that he may
run that readeth it. Habakkuk 2:2 KJV*

Most believers perform prophetic intercession on a regular basis.

As believers, we perform acts of symbolic prophetic
intercession on a regular basis, usually without realizing that
is what we are doing. We know that because the Lord has
instructed us in His Word to perform these acts, they are
powerful demonstrations that can change our lives and the
lives of others.

Communion

Jesus instructed us to act out this memorial of remembrance
to Him. We call it the Lord's Supper, or partaking of
communion.

*For I received from the Lord Himself that
[instruction] which I passed on to you, that the
Lord Jesus on the night in which He was betrayed
took bread; and when He had given thanks, He
broke it and said, "This is (represents) My body,
which is [offered as a sacrifice] for you." Do this
in remembrance of Me."In the same way, after
supper He took the cup, saying, "This cup is the
new covenant [ratified and established] in My
blood; do this, as often as you drink it, in [affec-
tionate] remembrance of Me."For every time you
eat this bread and drink this cup, you are
[symbolically] proclaiming [the fact of] the Lord's
death until He comes [again].
1 Corinthians 11:23-26*

The reason this would be called a prophetic action is that, as we perform communion, we are reminded of what Jesus said. We remember the past action of Jesus hanging on the cross as a sacrifice for our sins. This establishes the memorial of remembrance to Jesus. That past action makes it possible for us to do all things through Christ in our present time. We are prophetically looking to the future and proclaiming by our actions the facts of His death, resurrection, and His soon coming return. This act reconnects us to Yeshua-Jesus, the One who has given His life to ensure that we have the opportunity to live forever.

Water Baptism

Jesus began His ministry with the prophetic act of water baptism. At that time the Lord introduced the Holy Spirit symbolically, as a dove descending from heaven to land on Jesus.

After his baptism, as Jesus came up out of the water, the heavens were opened and he saw the Spirit of God descending like a dove and settling on him. And a voice from heaven said, "This is my dearly loved Son, who brings me great joy." Matthew 3:16-17 NLT

Today, the person being immersed in water baptism confesses out loud that they believe that Jesus Christ is the Son of God and that He died on the cross for their sins, that He was raised from the dead and is alive. Then the person baptizing them says something like this: "Upon your confession of faith in Jesus Christ, I baptize you in the name of the Father, the Son Jesus Christ, and the Holy Spirit." Then they lower the person under the water and as they are

70

bringing them back up out of the water they say something like, "And we raise you up to walk in newness of life."

Paul understood this death of the immersion and compared it to the death and resurrection of Yeshua Jesus.

> *Or are you ignorant of the fact that all of us who have been baptized into Christ Jesus were baptized into His death? We have therefore been buried with Him through baptism into death, so that just as Christ was raised from the dead through the glory* and *power of the Father, we too might walk* habitually *in newness of life [abandoning our old ways].* Romans 6:3-4

When we are baptized with water, it symbolizes that our old worldly minded flesh (our natured man) is dead, buried beneath the water. The new spiritual man that we just became through the baptism rises out of the water to walk in a new life.

This is a statement in the spiritual realm and a visible manifestation in the physical realm of your commitment to live this new spiritual life committed to Jesus. You make this committment to those watching. This is a rebirth into eternal life. Our physical lives will end on this earth, and we will walk through that thin veil and enter a new chapter of our lives. It will be a new life—one that will never end.

A prophetic act of anointing with oil

Anointing with oil is another symbolic act that speaks a message in the spiritual realm. As believers, we are instructed to call for the elders to anoint the sick with oil before praying for their healing.

Is anyone among you sick? He must call for the elders (spiritual leaders) of the church and they are to pray over him, anointing him with oil in the name of the Lord; and the prayer of faith will restore the one who is sick, and the Lord will raise him up; and if he has committed sins, he will be forgiven. James 5:14-15

And they were casting out many demons and were anointing with oil many who were sick, and healing them. Mark 6:13

Many churches still anoint the sick with oil as a symbolic act and pray for people to be healed.

There is a story in the Bible about a woman anointing Jesus with costly perfumed oil. Some commentaries say that the cost of the oil was a year's wages. She performed this prophetic act in a small group setting. Some commentaries say her reasoning must have been something like this; "I want to anoint Him as a sign of my adoration and love for Him." This woman was Mary, the sister of Lazarus.

As we read the story, it seems like this is just a woman pouring oil on Jesus, but upon reading the commentary we see it had a much deeper symbolic meaning. It was a prophetic act illustrating His soon coming death and burial.

Now when Jesus was [back] in Bethany, at the home of Simon the leper, a woman came to Him with an alabaster vial of very expensive perfume and she poured it on Jesus' head as He reclined at the table. But when the disciples saw it they were indig-nant and angry, saying, "Why all this waste [of money]? For this perfume might have been sold at a high price and the money given to the poor."But Jesus, aware [of the malice] of this [remark], said to them, "Why are you bothering the woman? She has done a good thing to Me. For you always have the poor with you; but you will not always have Me. When she poured this perfume on My body, she did it to prepare Me for burial. I assure you and most solemnly say to you, wherever this gospel [of salvation] is preached in the whole world, what this woman has done will also be told in memory of her [for her act of love and devotion]." Matthew 26:6-13

One commentary says,

"She did it for My burial." Not for the interment of His body, but for the preparation of His burial. Previous to burial, the Jews used to anoint their dead with spiced oil, to show their constant respect to the deceased, and their belief of the resurrection.

"They do all things necessary to the dead, but the body of Christ, when dead, was not to be so used: the women intended it, and prepared materials for it, but with the Sabbath coming on, they rested according to the commandment; They waited till the Sabbath was over; and early on the first day, in the morning, they came to the sepulcher, in order to do it, but it was too late, Christ was risen; the Holy Ghost directed her to this action, with this view, as it were, for the performing of these funeral rites before He was dead. By performing this symbolic act she didn't realize the implications or the prophetic significance of the act. Jesus wasn't deceased yet, but unknown to her within a few days He would be crucified and laid in the tomb. If she would have let her mind speak to her it might have talked her out of pouring this costly oil on Jesus. Logic would have led her wrong. Jesus would have been buried without the customary anointing performed for burial. [5]

There is always an element of timing involved that we should pay attention to. This story underlines that fact. She needed to do what she did on that exact day.

We can't underestimate the influence of one person. Mary performed her symbolic prophetic act in the living room of a home, but that act didn't end in that living room. It has continued to impact people all over the world. The Lord can use the smallest local group or congregation to play a vital part in His scheme of things when he wants to change a region territory or a nation for His purposes.

We see where Paul and Barnabas performed a prophetic act that impacted the people in the whole community of Corinth.

But the Jews incited the devout, prominent women and the leading men of the city, and instigated persecution against Paul and Barnabas, and drove them forcibly out of their district. But they shook

---

[5] Biblehub.com/commentaries/Matthew/26-12.htm

its dust from their feet in protest *against them and went to Iconium.* Acts 13:50-51.

Paul performed a prophetic act against another town.

> *But since the Jews kept resisting and opposing him, and blaspheming [God], he shook out his robe and said to them, "Your blood (damnation) be on your own heads! I am innocent of it. From now on I will go to the Gentiles."* Acts.18:6

The symbolic significance of the act as done by a Jew to Jews, no words and no act could so well express the Apostle's indignant protest. It was the last resource of one who found appeals to reason and conscience powerless, and was met by brute violence and clamor. [6]

The disciples didn't have the benefit of being able to see the future repercussions of their prophetic actions. As angry as Paul was, God used his frustration to bring the gospel to the Gentiles, which was God's plan. We are still thankful for that today.

---

[6] https://biblehub.com/commentariesacts/18-6.htm

*It is the glory of God to
conceal a matter, but
the glory of Kings is to
search out a matter.
Proverbs 25:2*

Chapter 6

Prophetic Dreams and Visions

Scripture reveals that dreams and visions are one of the main ways that God speaks to His people. He has used this method consistently throughout history. Sometimes it is to convey important revelation about what He needs the person to do for Him, or about what he is to perform in the future.

Definition of dream and visions

Dreams are a series of thoughts, images, and sensations occurring in a person's mind during sleep.

A vision is something seen in a dream, trance, or ecstasy especially a supernatural appearance that conveys a revelation.

People who specialize in dream interpretation say that a night vision can also be a vision within a dream. The difference between a vision and a dream is that you may forget the dream, but the vision will stay fresh in your mind. You can clearly recall the vision many years later because what you experienced was so real. The Lord uses both to get His point across.

> The Lord came down in a pillar of cloud and stood at the doorway of the Tabernacle, and he called Aaron and Miriam, and they came forward and He said, "Hear now my words:" If there is a prophet

among you, I the Lord will make myself know to him in a vision and I will speak to him in a dream. Numbers 12:5-6

The Lord makes a prophetic decree in Acts 2:17 concerning dreams and visions:

'And it shall be in the last days,' says God, 'That I will pour out My Spirit upon all mankind; and your sons and your daughters shall prophesy, and your young men shall see [divinely prompted] visions, and your old men shall dream [divinely prompted] dreams.

God wouldn't pour out His Spirit in this way if He wasn't planning on having the meanings and symbols shown in the dreams and visions interpreted.

The number of those who will be seeking a prophet to help them to know what God is saying to them through their dreams, is only going to increase as the future unfolds. God will need many people to assist Him. He will help us learn the symbolic language if we ask Him.

And they said to him, "We have [each] dreamed [distinct] dreams and there is no one to interpret them." So Joseph said to them, "Do not interpretations belong to God? Please tell me [your dreams]." Genesis 40:8

A word from God in a dream or vision can be symbolic or it can be literal, directing us to go in a specific direction to fulfill His purpose.

Now there was a disciple at Damascus named Ananias. The Lord said to him in a vision, "Ananias."

And he said, "Here I am, Lord." And the Lord said to him, "Rise and go to the street called Straight, and at the house of Judas look for a man of Tarsus named Saul, for behold, he is praying, and he has seen in a vision a man named Ananias come in and lay his hands on him so that he might regain his sight." Acts 9:10-12 ESV

And a vision appeared to Paul in the night: a man of Macedonia was standing there, urging him and saying, "Come over to Macedonia and help us." Acts 16:9 ESV

I once had a prophetic dream that changed my focus for an upcoming mission's trip. The dream alerted me to look for God's prophetic purpose in the trip so we could accomplish what He intended us to do. I was leaving the next day to go to Ghana, West Africa as part of a medical mission trip. We would be doing medical outreaches every day, and we would be taking turns preaching every night

In the dream, I had just walked out of a hospital and sat down in a wheelchair that was waiting for me in front of the hospital. There was a long driveway that curved along the front of the hospital. I began wheeling myself down that long driveway which would take me out to the main road that ran in front of the hospital. I noticed that I was wearing a pair of old fashioned nurse's shoes and was dressed in scrubs.

As I wheeled myself along, I noticed that I was going right down the middle of the road. A van came along behind me. The driver had to veer off the road to go around me. As the van went over a curb onto the grass, I turned and looked at the driver. I recognized him as a person who is known as a leader in the prophetic movement. I didn't know him personally. As we looked at each other, I saw that he had a look on his face of stern disappointment. Then I woke up.

I prayed for the Lord to show me what He wanted to tell me with the dream. I realized that He was saying that the man represented the prophetic realm, and God had used him as a point of contact for me to understand that this dream had to do with the prophetic assignment for Ghana. If I focused on the medical portion, I would cripple, or get off track of what God wanted us to do prophetically, on behalf of the people whom he loved so much, and for the country of Ghana. The dream was God's way of letting me know that the trip had a prophetic significance and to be alert for what He wanted us to accomplish while we were there.

The story of what happened on that trip is in the book I wrote, *From God's Hand to Your Land – Blessings*. I didn't share the dream in the book, but I do share what God told us to do and what we did prophetically to follow His directions. I included the results of what happened that we believe is a direct result of our actions to bless that nation.

Our team had a part to play on God's stage to affect the future of a nation. We might have missed it if we hadn't been praying for the Lord to give us information of what He wanted us to accomplish for His divine purposes while we were there.

God is no respector of persons. If you are willing, He will use you right where you are to affect nations through your prayers and actions.

Accessing God's glory through dreams and visions.

If the message in the dream or vision is hidden, it is up to us, the dreamer, to search it out. It is a responsibility that God gives us.

> It is the glory of God to conceal a matter, but the glory of Kings is to search out a matter.
> Proverbs 25:2

This is another way to access God's glory. We give Him the glory when we help someone understand their dreams and visions, with the help of our studies and the Holy Spirit. This is a supernatural ministry, and we, as believers, were created to live supernatural lives.

An exciting thing for us to know is that the Lord chooses all types of people to change the course of history through dreams and interpretation of dreams. He chooses people from all of economic backgrounds, from kings, to the seemingly least important people, such as a slave in a foreign land. The more serious we become about the interpretation of dreams and visions, the more mysteries the Lord will give us to solve.

We see in the following scripture it is important to acknowledge the Lord in every dream or vision that He gives us, because He is the one who gives us the interpretation.

> So he asked Pharaoh's officials who were in confinement with him in his master's house, "Why do you look so downhearted today? And they said to him," We have each dreamed (distinct) dreams and there is no one to interpret them. "So Joseph said to them, "Do not interpretations belong to God? Please tell me your dreams. Genesis 40:7-8

God will give dreams to those who aren't believers. In the story of Joseph, we saw that God will speak into the life of an unbeliever through dreams the same as He will speak to a believer in a dream.

How to become skilled at dream interpretation.

To become skilled at any type of work or activity requires special training and knowledge. If you are skilled at something, then you will have the knowledge and ability that will enable you to do it well. We can become skilled at understanding the symbolic language used in dreams and visions, but give the glory to the Lord for the interpretation.

The Bible tells us to study God's Word.

> *Study to shew thyself approved unto God, a workman that needeth not to be ashamed, rightly dividing the word of truth. 2 Timothy 2:15 KJV*

This is why it is important that we, as believers, learn this symbolic language so God can use us as He used Daniel, Joseph, and others. Every person is born with spiritual gifts from God. Whether they choose to use them for God or for other purposes is up to them. That is why we can receive a word of knowledge from someone who might be far from the Lord, and they may not even be aware at all that God just spoke to us through them.

King Nebuchadnezzar had a prophetic dream. (Daniel 2:1-23.) In the second year of his reign, Nebu-chadnezzar, King of Babylon, is troubled by a dream. He summons his magicians and astrologers and demands that they tell him what his dream was. They protest that no man can do such a thing, and King Nebuchadnezzar orders that they all be executed because they are frauds. Daniel hears the news of the impending executions that would include him and his friends, and they set their hearts to seek God for meaning of the dream.

Then the secret was revealed to Daniel in a vision of the night, and Daniel blessed the God of heaven. Daniel answered, "Blessed be the name of God forever and ever, For wisdom and power belong to Him. "It is He who changes the times and the seasons; He removes kings and establishes kings. He gives wisdom to the wise And [greater] knowledge to those who have understanding! "It is He who reveals the profound and hidden things; He knows what is in the darkness, And the light dwells with Him. "I thank You and praise You, O God of my fathers, for You have given me wisdom and power; even now You have made known to me what we requested of You, for You have made known to us [the solution to] the king's matter."
Daniel 2:19-23

Daniel tells the King the dream and saves the lives that were threatened to be put to death. The dream came true for King Nebuchadnezzar. God was giving him a warning, an opportunity to change his ways, but he apparently didn't want to pay attention to it. The fulfillment of the dream is shared in Daniel 4.

It is important to record what you feel that God is telling you or showing you.

According to scripture, if the dream or a word is from God it will surely come to pass. You may have to wait, but if you

83

endorse what you see in the dream or vision by recording it, then some type of divinely appointed messenger (called a *runner* in the scripture) can run with it. Apparently this runner will perform the behind the scenes work that needs to be done in preparation for the will of the Lord to come to pass.

> *I will stand upon my watch, and set me upon the tower, and will watch to see what he will say unto me, and what I shall answer when I am reproved. And the Lord answered me, and said, Write the vision, and make it plain upon tables, that he may run that readeth it. For the vision is yet for an appointed time, but at the end it shall speak, and not lie: though it tarry, wait for it; because it will surely come, it will not tarry.   Habakkuk 2:1-3*

You may have a vision and write it down, and someone in a future generation will read it and be used by God to fulfill His intended purposes for that generation.

The Lord gave Isaiah a prophetic word about the birth of Jesus almost 750 years ahead of His birth. If it hadn't been recorded, it couldn't have been used as one of the scriptures to prove that Yeshua/Jesus/Immanuel was the true Messiah. It was written down for future generations.

> *Therefore the Lord Himself will give you a sign: Listen carefully, the virgin will conceive and give birth to a son, and she will call his name Immanuel (God with us).   Isaiah 7:14*

The Word records the fulfillment years later, as the angel speaks with Mary in Luke 1:26-35. Mary was a young virgin who was engaged to Joseph when the angel Gabriel appeared to her. He spoke over her prophetically saying that she would bear a child.

> Then Mary said to the Angel, "How shall this be, seeing I have not laid with a man?" And the Angel answered," The Holy Ghost shall come upon you, and the power of the Highest shall overshadow you! Therefore that holy One which shall be born of you shall be called the Son Of God. (verse 34-35 KJV)

Isaiah also recorded the prophecy concerning the death of the Messiah.

> "Surely," he hath borne our griefs, and carried our sorrows...."He was wounded for our transgressions; he was bruised for our iniquities [wrongdoings]; ... and with his stripes we are healed." Isaiah 53:4–5. KJV

The Jews study the scriptures of Isaiah as he is one of their most beloved and revered prophets. But they are forbidden to study this particular scripture—Isaiah 53. I had an orthodox Jewish man tell me that once. I asked several Jewish people who had come to a belief in Jesus if this was true, and they assured me it was.

The escape to Egypt to save Jesus originated from a dream

If Joseph, the adoptive father of Jesus, wouldn't have acted on a dream after the birth of Jesus, future prophecy couldn't have been fulfilled. Of course, God has written the future so He knew Joseph would follow his dreams.

Now when they had gone, an angel of the Lord appeared to Joseph in a dream and said, "Get up! Take the Child and His mother and flee to Egypt, and remain there until I tell you; for Herod intends to search for the Child in order to destroy Him." So Joseph got up and took the Child and His mother while it was still night, and left for Egypt. He remained there until the death of Herod. This was to fulfill what the Lord had spoken by the prophet [Hosea]: "Out of Egypt I called My Son."
Matthew 2:13-23

Joseph was instantly obedient to the message in his dream. By his obedience the scripture would be fulfilled. It is more important to hear and obey the Lord than any other reason you think may keep you in right relationship with Him.

Then Joseph had another dream in which the Angel of the Lord told him to return to Israel with Jesus. He returned to Israel and was planning on going to Judea to settle, when he had another dream that changed his mind and his destination. He moved the family to Nazareth and fulfilled another prophetic word that was said: "He will be called a Nazarene."

When Herod died, an angel of the Lord suddenly appeared in a dream to Joseph in Egypt and said, 'Get up, take the child and his mother, and go to the land of Israel, for those who were seeking the child's life are dead. Then Joseph got up, took the child and his mother, and went to the land of Israel. But when he heard that Archelaus was ruling over Judea in place of his father Herod, he was afraid to go there. And after being warned in a dream, he went away to the district of Galilee. There he made his home in a town called Nazareth, so that what had been spoken through the prophets might be fulfilled, 'He will be called a Nazarene.'   Matthew 2:19-22 NLT

What if Joseph had decided not to act on his dreams and obey the angel that was sent to instruct him?

In this case, God told Joseph why he had to go to Egypt and again why he was to leave, but He doesn't always do that. Sometimes we only get part of the plan. In this case, because this one man followed the directions in the dream, it has affected the whole world and all of eternity forever.

We might have a two-way conversation with an angel or God in a dream.

In Solomon's dream, he not only heard from God but had a two-way conversation with Him.

At Gibeon the Lord appeared to Solomon in a dream by night; and God said, "Ask! What shall I give you?" And Solomon said: "You have shown great mercy to Your servant David my father, because he walked before You in truth, in righteousness, and in uprightness of heart with You; You have continued this great kindness for him, and You have given him a son to sit on his throne, as it is this day.

Now, O Lord my God, You have made Your servant king instead of my father David, but I am a little child; I do not know how to go out or come in. And Your servant is in the midst of Your people whom

You have chosen, a great people, too numerous to be numbered or counted. Therefore give to Your servant an understanding heart to judge Your people that I may discern between good and evil. For who is able to judge this great people of yours? 1 Kings 3:5-9 NKJV

Then Solomon awoke, and indeed it had been a dream. And he came to Jerusalem and stood before the ark of the covenant of the Lord, offered up burnt offerings, offered peace offerings, and made a feast for all his servants. I Kings 3:15 NKJV

My personal testimony of a two-way conversation in a vision within a dream.

One night I had a dream. I know now it was a vision within a dream because, even though it was many years ago, I remember it as if it were yesterday.

In the vision/dream, a man who looked to be about 30 years old walked up to me. I was standing in an area that looked like a desert. I knew I was in a different era in this dream because of the way the man was dressed. He had on a white robe with a blue sash and sandals. He was the size of an average man about 5'10". He had dark hair and a short beard. He approached me and smiled and said; "Hello Jeanette, my name is Phillip." He went on to say, "You have a question for me."

I didn't have a question, but I came up with the first thing that popped into my mind. I asked him, "How did you convince the Eunuch to believe you so quickly?" He smiled at me and brought one of his arms out from behind him. In his hand was a beautiful ornate silver chalice. As he extended his hand with the chalice in it he said, "With this." I looked inside the silver chalice and saw that it was full of clear sparkling water. I asked, "What is it?" He replied, "It is Living Water." Then he said, "Drink of it." I looked back at him and asked, "Can my husband drink of this?" He was smiling and nodded and said yes. Then I asked, "Can my children drink of this?" He responded again by smiling and nodding his head and saying, "Yes". Then I asked yet one more time; "Can my friends and anyone that I will ever meet and come to know drink of this Living Water?" He smiled very big at that and said "YES".

Instantly the scene in the vision changed. He was gone and I was standing on the shore of a very large lake, surrounded by the desert. I looked all around me and there appeared to be thousands of people behind and around me.

Suddenly I threw up my hands and yelled to everyone "Let's go." As I ran into the lake they all followed. I woke up and I was quite shaken. It was so real.

As I sought others who were skilled in dream interpretation, they said that the dream was telling me that the Lord had given me the gift of evangelism and teaching, much like Phillip had. The people I would minister to would be thirsty people, and I would bring them a drink of refreshing, life changing water.

I hadn't thought of myself as an evangelist at that time, but I had realized the Lord had given me a teaching gift. Now I focus on those two gifts and pray into them by decreeing I am a teacher and an evangelist com-missioned by the Lord. As a result of pursuing the vision/dream, the Lord has opened doors for me to bring many people to the life changing experience of accepting Jesus into their lives and experiencing the Living Water for themselves. I thank the Lord for that dream and for what it has meant to me.

Here is the story in the Bible about the apostle Phillip and his encounter with an angel giving him directions.

But an angel of the Lord said to Philip, "Get up and go south to the road that runs from Jerusalem down to Gaza." (This is a desert road). So he got up and went; and there was an Ethiopian eunuch [a man of great authority], a court official of Candace, queen of the Ethiopians, who was in charge of all her treasure. He had come to Jerusalem to worship, and he was returning, and sitting in his chariot he was reading [the scroll of] the prophet Isaiah.

Then the [Holy] Spirit said to Philip, "Go up and join this chariot." Philip ran up and heard the man reading the prophet Isaiah, and asked, "Do you understand what you are reading?" And he said, "Well, how could I [understand] unless someone guides me [correctly]?"

And he invited Philip to come up and sit with him. Now this was the passage of Scripture which he was reading: Like a sheep He was led to the slaughter; And as a lamb before its shearer is silent, So He does not open His mouth. "In humiliation His judgment was taken away [justice was denied Him].Who will describe His generation? For His life is taken from the earth."

The eunuch replied to Philip, "Please tell me, about whom does the prophet say this? About himself or about someone else?" Then Philip spoke and beginning with this Scripture he preached Jesus to him [explaining that He is the promised Messiah and the source of salvation].

As they continued along the road, they came to some water; and the eunuch exclaimed, "Look! Water! What forbids me from being baptized?" Philip said to him, "If you believe with all your heart, you may." And he replied, "I do believe that Jesus Christ is the Son of God." And he ordered that the chariot be stopped; and both Philip and the eunuch went down into the water, and Philip baptized him. When they came up out of the water, the Spirit of the Lord [suddenly] took Philip [and carried him] away [to a different place]; and the eunuch no longer saw him, but he went on his way rejoicing. But Philip found himself at Azotus, and as he passed through he preached the good news [of salvation] to all the cities, until he came to Caesarea [Maritima]. Acts 8:26-40

What an experience for Phillip! To interpret the Word, then get to baptize someone into the Kingdom of God, then fly away to another city without the use of a plane. After that dream I asked the Lord to translate me like He did Phillip! So far it hasn't happened. I get to fly, but so far it's been in a plane only, but someday I expect it to happen. In the meantime, I am stretching my faith to believe for it.

If you have a dream that causes concern.

It's important to make a determination as to the source of the dream or vision. Sometimes God will give us a warning dream about a future event that would appear to influence our lives in a negative way. We can't assume that just because we have a dream about something that it is God's will in the situation. We should be alert and try to avert the coming harm we are warned about, if possible. The least we can do is to pray into it in such a way as to either cancel it, or recognize that God is preparing us to go through a future event that won't be pleasant.

We see this in Acts. Paul must have been dealing with some fear. God was encouraging him not to be afraid of what was awaiting him.

> *And the Lord said to Paul one night in a vision, "Do not be afraid, but go on speaking and do not be silent." Acts 18:9 ESV*

If we receive a dream that appears to be futuristic or prophetic, we should come into agreement with it if we feel it is God's will. But sometimes we might not be sure if the dream is from God or the enemy.

I have heard of a person who dreamed they were in an automobile accident. If I felt that the Holy Spirit was revealing that the dream was a warning from Him, I would prophetically pray into the situation in such a way as to reaffirm that my life or anyone who was shown to be in the dream was in the hands of the Lord, and only His will would be accomplished. I would decree some scriptures over the people in the dream prophetically.

If a person hasn't committed their life to the Lord, He isn't responsible for them. They are fair game for the enemy; they are already in his camp. God will often use a dream to turn the life of an unbeliever around. The enemy isn't the only one who can use fear. The difference is that God uses it for a person's good, and He may use you as the agent of change in their life when you are able to interpret a dream or vision for them.

This is how I would pray over a negative dream. The prayer is written as if I had the dream. If the prayer is for another person who is asking you to pray for them, change the language to fit your needs.

> Dear Heavenly Father, I lift this dream to You. If this is a warning from You to pray into my coming future, then here is my prayer. I thank You that You say in Jeremiah 29:11, *For I know the plans and thoughts that I have for you,' says the Lord, 'plans for peace and well-being and not for disaster, to give you a future and a hope.* I thank You that my future is in Your hands and You control what might happen.

> I also decree Psalm 31:14-16 over myself: But as for me, I trust [confidently] in You and Your greatness, O Lord; I said, "You are my God." My times are in Your hands; Rescue me from the hand of my enemies and from those who pursue and persecute me. Make Your face shine upon Your servant; Save me in Your lovingkindness. I thank You for Your Word that says the angel of the Lord encamps around those who fear Him [with awe-inspired reverence and worship Him

with obedience], and He rescues [each of] them. (Psalm 34:7) I receive Your Words and apply them to my life. I decree that if this dream is from the enemy to bring fear upon me, I rebuke it right now in the name of Jesus. I decree that the negative things I saw in the dream shall never come to pass. It is cancelled and I pray crop failure over it. Amen.

At other times, a dream may contain an answer for a person and shows them a picture, in symbolic form, of what they are currently going through. In that case, it can bring a person peace knowing that God sees what they are going through, and it may contain a directive from Him that can help them to know how to pray.

This is another example of God speaking to a man in a dream and giving him words of knowledge.

> One of his servants said, "None [of us is helping him], my lord, O king; but Elisha, the prophet who is in Israel, tells the king of Israel the words that you speak in your bedroom." 2 Kings 6:12

Having the same dream

If a person has a similar dream two nights in a row, the scripture says that it will come to pass quickly.

> That the dream was repeated twice to Pharaoh [and in two different ways] indicates that this matter is fully determined and established by God, and God will bring it to pass very quickly. Genesis 41:32

For God speaks once, and even twice, yet no one notices it (including you, Job.) In a dream, a vision of the night (one may hear God's voice) when deep sleep falls on men, while slumbering upon the bed. Job 33:14-15

Developing our spiritual senses

Here are some ways in which we can develop our spiritual senses to receive a dream, vision, or word of direction from the Lord. Because God is Spirit, He speaks a spiritual language. It is seen and heard by our spirit so it makes sense to want to develop that part of ourselves.

We develop our ability to recognize a word from God by training ourselves. It helps to develop a practice of quieting yourself, maybe playing some quiet worship music which will prepare the atmosphere. Worship and praise opens the heavens over us. Listen for Him to speak to you or give some type of impression. This is called soaking in His presence. Don't try to force anything. Focus on the Lord and ask Him for revelation. It can also help to read the Bible while you are meditating on the Lord in this way.

There are ministries that teach classes on dream and vision interpretation. Several of them activate their students after training by going into malls and new age fairs. They set up tables or booths and interpret dreams for people. This has provided a way to reach people that ordinarily may not be open to the gospel. Many of these people have come to know the Lord through this unique type of evangelism

There are many books that also teach this vocabulary of symbolic language. God has given us every opportunity to learn His language of symbolism.

These are just a few ideas. We can't limit the ways that God speaks to us. There have been times in my life when He spoke something profound to me that changed my life, right in the midst of my day. I wasn't even focused on Him. Our mission is to seek the Lord about our dreams, to study the dream language, and when we think we have an answer, pray about it. As prophetic people, we are as kings before the Lord and this is our responsibility.

If you would like to receive dreams and visions from the Lord, and would like to interpret them properly, you should speak His work prophetically over yourself. By rehearsing the scriptures over yourself in thankful agreement with Him, you can be sure you are in agreement with His will for your life. When we decree God's Word over ourselves, it is as if He is ordering it to come to pass in our lives. This is how we give His word a voice on the earth.

Here is an example of a prayer and prophetic decree you can pray over yourself concerning dreams/visions and their interpretation:

> Dear Heavenly Father,
> I thank You that according to Your Word in Acts 2:17, *You are pouring out Your spirit upon all flesh*. I receive this flow of dreams and visions from Your Holy Spirit upon my life. I repent for not placing more importance on the dreams or visions that You have given me in the past, and ask that You forgive me. I ask that You bless me with godly wisdom and knowledge that will help me to interpret the dreams and vision You will pour out upon me, all for Your glory.

I speak to my heart and say, You are a prepared heart ready to perform the will of the Lord. I declare that my ears will hear and my eyes will see what You are telling me. I will grow and increase in spiritual understanding. I look forward to learning to interpret dreams and visions, for Your glory.

I remind You that You gave Daniel insight and revelation, with wisdom and understanding to understand the symbolic language You use in dreams and visions. I proclaim Your word over myself and thank You that You desire for Your Word to be applied to my life. I will commit myself to seek the Holy Spirit, to study and learn Your symbolic language, and I will give You all the glory, just as Daniel did when You revealed the secrets of interpretation to him. *Then the secret was revealed to Daniel in a night vision. So Daniel blessed the God of heaven. (Daniel 2)*

Thank You so much for hearing my petition. I love hearing from You in whatever way You choose to talk to me. You are my Father and I love connecting with You every day. In Jesus name. Amen.

I declare over myself, in agreement with Psalm 37:4-5: I delight myself in the Lord, and He will give me the desires and petitions of my heart. I commit my way to the Lord; I trust in Him and He will do it.

*For we are his workmanship, created
in Christ Jesus for good works, which
God prepared beforehand, that we
should walk in them.
Ephesians 2:10 NKJV*

Chapter 7

Prophetic Artisans

Singers, Musicians, Dancers, Artists and Writers

Having gifts that differ according to the grace given to us, let us use them: if prophecy, in proportion to our faith. Romans 12:6 ESV

This scripture is speaking of prophecy as one of the gifts of the Holy Spirit. It is addressed to any believer who asks the Lord for the gift of prophecy, then begins to develop that gift by speaking or demonstrating what the Lord is saying to them under the anointing of the Holy Spirit.

It is the will of the Lord that every believer seek out this gift. 1 Corinthians 14:5 says, "I wish you could all speak in tongues, but even more I wish you could all prophesy..." and again in 1 Corinthians 14:39, "So my dear brothers and sisters, be eager to prophesy..." (NLT)

If you are a singer, musician, dancer, artist, or writer, the gift you operate in, whether you recognize it or not, has an important role to play in prophetic intercession. It is to be used to fulfill God's prophetic purposes. Your gift comes with a specially designed anointing that is just for you.

For we are his workmanship, created in Christ Jesus for good works, which God prepared beforehand, that we should walk in them. Ephesians 2:10 NKJV

99

The anointing assigned to each artisan believer is infused with a mantle of a specific calling that rests upon their life. Every one of these artisan gifts are intertwined with worship which is interwoven with intercession.

That means a person on the worship team is an intercessor. Many people do not utilize the opportunity of worship and praise to intercede. They go about their ministry to the Lord with what they are best at, without applying the intercession that could be so effective in their lives and the lives of others.

This story relates how a group of people listened to the prophetic word given by the levitical priest (which means he was an intercessor) and won a battle that saved the nation of Israel with praise and worship as their only weapons.

> Then the Spirit of the Lord came on Jahaziel son of Zechariah, the son of Benaiah, the son of Jeiel, the son of Mattaniah, a Levite and descendant of Asaph, as he stood in the assembly. He said: "Listen, King Jehoshaphat and all who live in Judah and Jerusalem! This is what the Lord says to you: 'Do not be afraid or discouraged because of this vast army. For the battle is not yours, but God's. Tomorrow march down against them. They will be climbing up by the Pass of Ziz, and you will find them at the end of the gorge in the Desert of Jeruel. You will not have to fight this battle. Take up your positions; stand firm and see the deliverance the Lord will give you, Judah and Jerusalem. Do not be afraid; do not be discouraged. Go out to face them tomorrow, and the Lord will be with you." Jehoshaphat bowed

down with his face to the ground, and all the people of Judah and Jerusalem fell down in worship before the Lord. Then some Levites from the Kohathites and Korahites stood up and praised the Lord, the God of Israel, with a very loud voice.

Early in the morning they left for the Desert of Tekoa. As they set out, Jehoshaphat stood and said, "Listen to me, Judah and people of Jerusalem! Have faith in the Lord your God and you will be upheld; have faith in his prophets and you will be successful."

After consulting the people, Jehoshaphat appointed men to sing to the Lord and to praise him for the splendor of his holiness as they went out at the head of the army, saying: "Give thanks to the Lord, for his love endures forever." As they began to sing and praise, the Lord set ambushes against the men of Ammon and Moab and Mount Seir who were invading Judah, and they were defeated. The Ammonites and Moabites rose up against the men from Mount Seir to destroy and annihilate them. After they finished slaughtering the men from Seir, they helped to destroy one another.

When the men of Judah came to the place that overlooks the desert and looked toward the vast army, they saw only dead bodies lying on the ground; no one had escaped. So Jehoshaphat and his men went to carry off their plunder, and they found among them a great amount of equipment *and clothing and also articles of value—more than they could take away. There was so much plunder that it took three days to collect it. On the fourth day they assembled in the Valley of Berakah, where they praised the Lord. This is why it is called the Valley of Berakah to this day.*

Then, led by Jehoshaphat, all the men of Judah and Jerusalem returned joyfully to Jerusalem, for the Lord had given them cause to rejoice over their enemies. They entered Jerusalem and went to the temple of the Lord with harps and lyres and trumpets.

The fear of God came on all the surrounding kingdoms when they heard how the Lord had fought against the enemies of Israel. And the kingdom of Jehoshaphat was at peace, for his God had given him rest on every side.
2 Chronicles 20:14-29 NIV

The praise and worship sent total confusion into the enemy camp. I can't imagine the trust the people must have had in Jehosaphat to have gone to battle without weapons! They were trained to fight, but like the battle of Jericho, God didn't allow them to use their weapons. When we aren't allowed by God to use any of our personal arsenal of expertise in our own gifts, God gets the glory.

Another scripture that ties worship and intercession together is Psalm 149:6-9 (NKJV).

Let the high praises of God be in their mouth...to execute vengeance (justice) on the nations, and punishments on the peoples; to bind their kings with chains and their nobles with fetters of iron, to execute on them the written judgment--this honor have all His saints.

An example of a musician playing worship music as a tool for deliverance.

We see in the scripture when David played on the harp in the presence of King Saul, it caused a deliverance to come upon King Saul. Demons fled and he would calm down when David played the harp for him.

So it came about that whenever the [evil] spirit from God was on Saul, David took a harp and played it with his hand; so Saul would be refreshed and be well, and the evil spirit would leave him.
1 Samuel 16:23

The prophets in the Bible understood that worship was the key to an open heaven and God's favor. Following are some more examples of how God can use musicians, singers and dancers to welcome His presence and release a spirit of prophecy into the midst.

And it came to pass as they came, when David was returned from the slaughter of the Philistine, that the women came out of all cities of Israel, singing and dancing, to meet king Saul, with tabrets, with joy, and with instruments of music, and the women answered one another as they played, and said, Saul hath slain his thousands, and David his ten thousands. And Saul was very wroth, and the saying displeased him; and he said, they have ascribed unto David ten thousands, and to me they have ascribed but thousands: and what can he have more but the kingdom? And Saul eyed David from that day and forward.   1 Samuel 18:6-9 KJV

At that time, David had only killed Goliath, a lion and a bear. The Spirit of Prophecy came upon them as they worshipped with their instruments and they prophesied that David was greater than Saul, who was king at the time. The musicians and the dancers welcomed and ushered in the Spirit of Prophecy.

In this next scripture, the prophet Samuel is telling King Saul to go over to the high place of Gibeon, and then he prophesies that if Saul gets into their midst he will begin to prophecy too.

After that you will come to the hill of God where the garrison of the Philistines is; and when you come there to the city, you will meet a group of prophets coming down from the high place [of worship] with harp, tambourine, flute, and lyre before them, and they will be prophesying. Then the Spirit of the LORD will come upon you mightily, and you will prophesy with them, and you will be changed into another man. 1 Samuel 10:5-6

We see this pattern in modern days in the Houses of Prayer that are in our nation and internationally. The worshippers are being taught how to hear the voice of the Lord while playing their instruments and singing praises. They prophesy through their songs, singing as the Holy Spirit gives them words to release.

Elisha said, "As the LORD of hosts (armies) lives, before whom I stand, were it not that I have regard for Jehoshaphat king of Judah, I would not look at you nor see you [king of Israel]. But now bring me a musician." And it came about while the musician played, that the hand (power) of the LORD came upon Elisha. He said, "Thus says the LORD, 'Make this valley (the Arabah) full of trenches.' For thus says the LORD, 'You will not see wind or rain, yet that valley will be filled with water, so you and your cattle and your other animals may drink. This is but a simple thing in the sight of the LORD; He will also hand over the Moabites to you. You shall strike every fortified city and every choice (principal) city, and cut down every good tree and stop up all sources of water, and ruin every good piece of land with stones.'" It happened in the morning, when the sacrifice was offered, that suddenly water came [miraculously] from the area of Edom, and the country was filled with water. 2 Kings 3:14-20

Judah means *praise*. The presence of God is in the praise.

And all of the Levitical singers, Asaph, Heman, and Jeduthun, with their sons and relatives, clothed in fine linen, with cymbals, harps, and lyres were standing at the east end of the altar, and with them a hundred and twenty priests blowing trumpets in unison when the trumpeters and singers were to make themselves heard with one voice praising and thanking the LORD, and when they raised their voices accompanied by the trumpets and cymbals and [other] instruments of music, and when they praised the LORD, saying, "For He is good, for His mercy and loving kindness endure forever," then

*the house of the LORD was filled with a cloud, so
that the priests could not remain standing to
minister because of the cloud; for the glory and
brilliance of the LORD filled the house of God.*
2 Chronicles 5:12-14

During praise and worship there is always an open heaven.
It makes communication between us and God easier. It's
very common to get a download of prophetic inspiration
while at any type of gathering where worship or praise is
playing. It is good to be prepared by having paper and pen
handy. Sometimes we will receive a word or instruction to
perform a prophetic act and it's good to be prepared.

If we feel we are too shy or afraid to step out and perform
a prophetic act, the story of Gideon should serve to make
us thankful and willing to activate whatever courage we can
find within ourselves to perform the thing the Lord might
ask of us. Gideon was about as fearful as a person could be.
God told him through an angel that he would use him to
save Israel. Gideon argued with the angel of the Lord that
he wouldn't be able to do that.

*But Gideon said to Him, "Please Lord, how am I to
rescue Israel? Behold, my family is the least
[significant] in Manasseh, and I am the youngest
(smallest) in my father's house." Judges 6:15*

But the angel of the Lord convinced Gideon that, with the
help of the Lord, he could rescue a whole nation from the
encircling armies. Gideon went on to get the credit for
setting Israel free from their enemies. The story is found in
Judges 6-8. After reading that story, one shouldn't feel

fearful about the small things that God may ask us to do, compared to what He has asked people to do in the past.

Artists

I found the following article online that explains the effect of art on people.

> As people interact with our creative work in whatever media, a conversation of sorts begins where the God of the universe begins to speak to the heart of the viewer. It is in that moment that our art becomes a conduit for the power and presence of God to impact the life of another in a way that is both powerful and subtle. Suddenly, the viewer becomes enraptured in a divine conversation with the one who created them, all because an artist chose to cooperate with the Holy Spirit in their creative expression. Have you ever tried to share the Gospel with someone that just wasn't ready to hear it, for whatever reason? Maybe baggage from the past, fear or even misunderstanding keeps them from receiving the free gift of God through Jesus. On the other hand, you may see that same person listen to a song, watch a movie or see a painting that has a profound effect on them emotionally and spiritually, causing them to make a life change, deal with a difficult issue or even have a change of heart.
>
> Why? Because art was specifically designed by the Father to bypass common barriers like intellect, fear, and self-protection, going right to

the core of a person's spirit, obviously, this can be used by the enemy as well, but when your art is infused with the power and presence of God, it can literally be a conduit to heal emotions, transform hearts and even shift culture. [7]

A person sees a work of art and it can help them see things in a new way. It can transport them emotionally back in time, or help them envision a future event.

Artists and interior designers have long understood that color can dramatically affect moods, feelings, and emotions. Color is a powerful communication tool and can be used to signal action, influence, mood, and even influence physiological reactions.

Writers

Without writers we wouldn't have our Bible. We wouldn't have the songs of the Psalms. If God has given you something to write, then it is important to Him that you do it. If you recognize the importance of it in God's eyes you will have the faith to complete the work. God will open the doors for you to get your God-inspired work published.

People I have met have said that God told them they would write a book, but they aren't doing anything about it except saying that God told them to do it. Remember, when we stand before Him, He will ask what we did with what He gave us to do.

A person may feel their life is in a holding pattern and can't figure out why they don't seem to get ahead. Another year passes and nothing has changed for them. They must ask

---

[7] http://www.theworshipstudio.org/what-is-prophetic-art.html

themselves if there is something they felt the Lord told them to do that they haven't done.

I know this scripture isn't about writing, but I want to encourage you to write if God has told you to.

> Then Mordecai told them to reply to Esther, "Do not imagine that you in the king's palace can escape any more than all the Jews. For if you remain silent at this time, liberation and rescue will arise for the Jews from another place, and you and your father's house will perish [since you did not help when you had the chance]. And who knows whether you have attained royalty for such a time as this [and for this very purpose]?" Esther 4:13-14.

I have had people tell me when some new revelation comes out for the body of Christ, that God had told them the revelation years ago. When I ask them if they wrote it down they said no. God gives people opportunities, and if they don't take them, He will give the revelation to someone who will get the job done.

When God tells a person to do something and the person argues themselves out of it because they say they don't have the talent or the resources to do what God has asked them to do, He sees that as pride. When a person looks to their own abilities and resources to be able to do what He is asking of them, they forget that He wants to be their provider. In most of the stories, God purposely asked people to do things they weren't capable of doing so He would get the glory.

Thus says the Lord, the God of Israel, 'Write all the words which I have spoken to you in a book.' Jeremiah 30:2

My heart overflows with a good theme; I address my psalm to the King. My tongue is like the pen of a skillful writer. Psalm 45:1

Chapter 8

We Remember— Then We Demonstrate!

Rehearsing the Word in demonstration is not a religious ritual, but an act of devotion and a memorial of remembrance.

This type of memorial has been echoed by believers throughout the centuries. We can learn by reading examples of how God's people made prophetic declarations of remembrance that caught God's attention and caused Him to respond on their behalf. They would praise and exalt Him for the wonderful deeds that He performed in the past, thus bringing Him glory in the present.

Psalm 136 is all about giving the Lord thanksgiving and praise because of His loving kindness and mercy. Every verse praises God for a different blessing, and ends with the words, *'His mercy endures forever.'*

Here are a few scriptures, out of the many, that instruct us to remind the Lord of His goodness and of His great acts on our behalf.

> *Remember [with gratitude] His marvelous deeds which He has done, His miracles and the judgments from His mouth. 1 Chronicles 16:12*

> *Remember the former things of old; for I am God, and there is no other; I am God, and there is none like me. Isaiah 46:9 NKJV*

I will (solemnly) remember the deeds of the Lord;
yes, I will (wholeheartedly) remember your wonder
of old.   Psalm 77:11

The word *remember* means to keep an image or idea in your mind of something or someone from the past; to not forget something; to make a memorial.

As we bring the acts of God to *remembrance*, we breathe life into the scripture. This will please God. We are welcoming the Spirit of Prophecy into our midst, and His glory will change our atmosphere and affect our own attitude at the same time.

The trumpeters and singers performed together in
unison to praise and give thanks to the LORD.
Accompanied by trumpets, cymbals, and other
instruments, they raised their voices and praised
the LORD with these words: "He is good! His
faithful love endures forever!" At that moment a
thick cloud filled the Temple of the LORD. The
priests could not continue their service because of
the cloud, for the glorious presence of
the LORD filled the Temple of God.
2 Chronicles 5:13-14 NLT

Our faith will grow. Discouragement and fear will flee as the Word of God is released. I can remember when our children were young, a friend and I would get on the phone and quote the Word over them. She would read a scripture and then I would read a scripture. After several scriptures, the enemy had listened to all he could take and he left. It was amazing to feel the transformation. Our attitudes changed. Faith rushed in and drove out any fear over what our children were going through. The enemy couldn't get away from us quick enough.

The Lord sends His warring angels.

This story is a good example of what occurs when people repent for their sins, then remind God of His mighty acts that He performed on their behalf in the past. One of the great things about this story is that it includes His response to the people, which is an encouragement to each of us.

We read in Judges 4:1-5,31, that Israel was facing a battle that threatened to wipe out their very existence. The scripture explains that the people of Israel were put into bondage for following foreign gods. But they cried out to the Lord and He felt compassion for them when He heard their cries. He positioned a righteous judge and prophetess to lead them in repentance and restoration.

At the time of this story, the people of Israel had been prisoners in their own land for 20 years. They were afraid to risk their lives by even walking along the roads outside of the city gates. The scripture records that they didn't have any weapons with which to defend themselves. Deborah's song describes their situation: *"Was there a shield or spear seen among 40,000?"* (Judges 5:8b)

Then God spoke through Deborah and said it was time to fight for their freedom, but He would go ahead of them and defeat their enemies. After hearing from God, she called for and prophesied to Israel's General Barak. She told him that it was time to go to war against their oppressors.

> *The Lord says, "I will draw out Sisera, the commander of Jabin's army, with his chariots and*

*his infantry to meet you at the river Kishon, and I
will hand him over to you." Judges 4:7*

Barak was fearful, and he told her that he would only do it if she would come with him. She agreed, but prophesied that he wouldn't get credit for the winning of the battle but that a woman would. She then prophesied again to encourage him to go to war and trust God.

*Deborah said to Barak "Arise! for this is the day
when the Lord has given Sisera into your hand. Has
the Lord not gone out before you?" Judges 4:14*

So, Barak agreed to go, but before they went out to fight, the scripture records that Deborah led the villagers to "the quiet places of drawing water." There she presents her case before the Lord and the people.

She stated why Israel was in such a terrible state. She said, *"They chose new gods, then there was war in the gates."* *(Judges 5:8)* She is confessing the sin that caused God to turn His back on them.

The location she chose to assemble the people before God was strategic. Historically, when the nation of Israel sinned against God, one of the ways they demonstrated to Him in a symbolic way that they had repentant hearts, was to go to a place for drawing water (such as a well) and repent before God, then draw the water and pour it out on the ground. We find examples of this.

*Samuel said, "Gather all Israel together at Mizpah
and I will pray to the LORD for you." So they
gathered at Mizpah, and drew water and poured it
out before the LORD, and fasted on that day and*

said there, "We have sinned against the LORD." And Samuel judged the Israelites at Mizpah.
1 Samuel 7:5-6

Arise, cry out in the night, at the beginning of the watches of the night; pour out your heart like water before the presence of the LORD. Lift up your hands to him for the lives of your little ones who faint from hunger at the head of every street.
Lamentations 2:19

The Word says that Deborah and Barak followed by singing a prophetic song:

"Hear this, you kings! Listen, you rulers! I, even I, will sing to the LORD; I will praise the LORD, the God of Israel, in song." Judges 5:3 NIV

It seems that she is addressing and prophesying a warning to spiritual forces in high places. They hadn't gone into battle yet, and the human foreign rulers certainly weren't present at their repentance and praise session.

They went on to prophesy a big storm, as God had done before.

When you, LORD, went out from Seir, when you marched from the land of Edom, the earth shook, the heavens poured, the clouds poured down water. The mountains quaked before the LORD, the One of Sinai, before the Lord, the God of Israel.
Judges 5:4 NIV

Then they went out to battle. The Word says that, after their repentance and memorial service they went down to the city gates. Then according to the Word, the angelic warfare began. A mighty storm blew up.

> *Kings came, they fought, the kings of Canaan fought. At Taanach, by the waters of Megiddo, they took no plunder of silver. Judges 5:19 NIV*

This could be describing a spiritual battle between principalities over the region and the heavenly host. Angels or spiritual entities have no need for earthly spoil. Scripture goes on to say:

> *From the heavens the stars fought, from their courses they fought against Sisera. The river Kishon swept them away, the age-old river, the river Kishon. March on, my soul; be strong! then thundered the horses' hooves galloping, galloping go his mighty steeds. Judges 5:20 NIV*

The Lord confused and terrified Sisera and all his chariot drivers and all his army. And Sisera alighted from his chariot and fled on foot.

The battle began to turn. It has been speculated that Sisera and his troops were being swept away as they tried to cross the river to attack. The enemy troops began to flee. Sisera, their General, was trying to escape capture. He came to the tent of a man named Heber, who was a friend of the Canaanite king. Herber's wife, Jael, met him at the door to the tent. He trusted her and asked her to hide him so he could rest.

Because of the culture at that time, he was sure he would be safe. A man wouldn't be caught in the tent with the wife of another man without the husband being there. Sisera knew that if he hid in her tent and she told those searching for him that no man was there, they would believe her and not search the tent.

She assured him he would be safe, and offered him a cup of milk before he laid down to rest. The Bible says that he felt so safe he fell sound asleep. She saw her opportunity and took it. She drove a tent peg through the temple of the unsuspecting Sisera and killed him

She was an undercover intercessor for Israel. We never know where God has planted people strategically. As intercessors, we never know when we may be able to do something for God that can affect a nation.

When Barak arrived at her tent, she showed him his enemy who lay dead. She got the credit for winning the battle for Israel, which fulfilled Deborah's prophecy. At the end of the song, Deborah praises the brave Jael for having, with her own hand, killed the worst of Israel's enemies. She concludes her song of praise to God with these words:

> *Blessed above women shalt Jael be, The wife of Heber the Kenite, above women in the tent shall she be blessed...At her feet he sank, he fell, he lay; At her feet he sank, he fell; Where he sank, there he fell dead...So perish all thine enemies, O God; But they that love Him be as the sun going forth in its might. Judges 5:24,27,31 KJV*

Who is [He then] this King of glory? The Lord of hosts, He is the King of glory [who rules over all creation with His heavenly armies].
Psalm 24:10

Chapter 9

Prophetic Intercession with Angelic Intervention

This chapter is a tribute to the Lord, and to the angelic forces that stand ready to perform His commands. Angels are always working behind the scenes to bring the future to pass.

Biblical history reveals that hundreds of years in advance of the fulfillment of a prophetic word, God is weaving all things together to bring His word to fulfillment. It may seem as if nothing is happening to bring your vision to pass, but if it came from God and you write it down and pray into it, you can be assured that there is work going on behind the scenes. When it seems like God has forgotten, it can suddenly come to pass.

There is a scripture that tells us of such a time.

> *Son of Man, behold, the House of Israel is saying, 'The vision that Ezekiel sees is for many years from now, and he prophesies of the times that are far off." Therefore, say to them, "Thus say the LORD God, "None of my words will be delayed any longer. Whatever word I speak will be fulfilled completely," says the LORD God.   Ezekiel 12:27-28*

God doesn't see His Word as being delayed even if we might. He has an appointed time. It may not be our time.

Then the LORD replied: "Write down the revelation and make it plain on tablets so that a herald may run with it. Habakkuk 2:2 NIV

I used this translation because it says *a herald will run with it.* A hearld is someone who announces something. We know that the angel Gabriel announced to Mary that she was with child and when he was born to name him Emmanuel. He announced or heralded to Zechariah the coming birth of his son who was to be called John. Gabriel was instructed by God to explain Daniel's vision to him.

God's relationship with angels

God is referred to as the "Lord of Hosts" throughout scripture.

O LORD God of Heaven's Armies! Where is there anyone as mighty as you, O LORD? You are entirely faithful. You rule the oceans. You subdue their storm-tossed waves. Psalm 89:8-9 NLT

The LORD thunders at the head of his army; his forces are beyond number, and mighty is the army that obeys his command. The day of the LORD is great; it is dreadful. Who can endure it? Joel 2:11 NIV

Who is [He then] this King of glory? The Lord of hosts, He is the King of glory [who rules over all creation with His heavenly armies]. Psalm 24:10

"Yahweh-Sabaoth" in Hebrew means "The Lord of Armies," which reflects His position and power over both spiritual and physical armies.

120

Can man direct angels to perform on God's behalf?

I have been in conferences and at prayer gatherings and have heard people directing and commanding angels to go places and do things that the person tells them to do. There doesn't seem to be any scriptures that could provide an example to support the theory that humans are to give angels commands. There are many scriptures that say that God Himself instructs the angels.

As the Lord of the Heavenly Hosts, He has an unbeatable army ready to fight on our behalf. He is the Commander of that army. They listen for His instructions and they go to perform it. He has given us the option of quoting His Word, and the angels respond to it and go forth to perform it. We can make our appeal to God and He will send angels to work on our behalf.

> Bless the Lord, ye his angels, that excel in strength, that do his commandments, hearkening unto the voice of his Word. Bless ye the Lord, all his hosts; ye ministers of his that do his pleasure. Bless the Lord all his works in all places of his dominion. Bless the Lord, O my soul. Psalm 103:20-22 KJV

As we compare our military on the earth to the heavenly army, we know they operate the same. As a civilian, I wouldn't try to command anyone in the military because they wouldn't respond to my orders. If I were to go to their commander and make my appeal to him, there is a chance that he would assign someone to help me out.

I am including some scriptures that show that the people of the Bible appealed to God in their distress, and He sent angels to intervene on their behalf.

But when we cried out to the LORD (for help) He heard us and sent an angel and brought us out of Egypt. Numbers 20:16

Shadrach, Meshach, and Abednego refused to bow down to Nebuchadnezzar's image. They were thrown in a fiery furnace. God in his mercy, *"sent his angel and rescued his servants!"* (see Daniel 3:28)

God "sent his angel" to deliver Daniel from the mouths of the lions in their den. (see Daniel 6:22)

God sent an angel in response to the prayers of the church on behalf of Peter who was in chains in prison. When Peter was delivered, he testified,

"Now I know without a doubt that the Lord sent his angel and rescued me from Herod's clutches and from everything the Jewish people were anticipating." Acts 12:11 NIV

I'm not judging anyone who does command angels. My concern is that without scriptural validation, the person who commands angels might presume that angels are going forth to follow their commands, but they may not receive their expected result. The concern is for the person who is a new believer; disappointment could open a door for unbelief to come in.

Angels tell us that they are fellow servants with us. As servants they follow the directions of their master.

Then I fell down at his feet to worship him, but he [stopped me and] said to me, "You must not do that; I am a fellow servant with you and your

brothers and sisters who have and hold the
testimony of Jesus.   Revelation 19:10

We read of how the Lord sent an angel before Moses to help
him as the Israelites went in to conquer their enemies and
take possession of their promised land. In the following
scriptures, God assures Moses that He will assign angelic
assistance to the Israelites as they go on their journey. This
reveals a perfect demonstration of divinity and humanity
working together.

> "Behold, I am going to send an Angel before you
> to keep and guard you on the way and to bring you
> to the place I have prepared. Be on your guard
> before Him, listen to and obey His voice; do not be
> rebellious toward Him or provoke Him, for He will
> not pardon your transgression, since My Name
> (authority) is in Him. But if you will indeed listen
> to and truly obey His voice and do everything that
> I say, then I will be an enemy to your enemies and
> an adversary to your adversaries.
> Exodus 23:20-22

As angels proceed to fulfill their orders from the Lord, they
are busy with an ongoing mission to minister to us today, to
assist us in fulfilling our prophetic assignments and move us
along in our destinies.

Angels are ageless spirits, so the one helping you today may
be the same one who helped King David in his day. This
promise is for each of us. We are all on a journey and God
will assign angels to help us. Hebrews 1:14 assures us that
the Lord will send us angelic help from heaven. Are not all
the angels ministering spirits sent out [by God] to serve

[accompany, protect] those who will inherit salvation? [Of course they are!]

Do people have conversations with angels?

There are many scriptures that tell stories of people speaking with angels. Here are a few examples of angels speaking to men.

Then an angel of the Lord appeared to him, standing at the right side of the altar of incense. When Zechariah saw him, he was startled and was gripped with fear. But the angel said to him: "Do not be afraid, Zechariah; your prayer has been heard. Your wife Elizabeth will bear you a son, and you are to call him John.   Luke 1:11-13 NIV

As they entered the tomb, they saw a young man dressed in a white robe sitting on the right side, and they were alarmed. "Don't be alarmed," he said. "You are looking for Jesus the Nazarene, who was crucified. He has risen! He is not here. See the place where they laid him. But go, tell his disciples and Peter, 'He is going ahead of you into Galilee. There you will see him, just as he told you.'"
Mark 16:5-7 NIV

They were looking intently up into the sky as he was going, when suddenly two men dressed in white stood beside them. "Men of Galilee," they said, "Why do you stand here looking into the sky? This same Jesus, who has been taken from you into heaven, will come back in the same way you have seen him go into heaven.   Acts 1:10-11 NIV

My personal testimony of an angelic visitation.

I know that, according to the scriptures, the appearance of an angel can be overwhelming. But I have learned over the years that they can be very personable. I am always hearing testimonies from others of how angels have ministered to them, so I decided to share my angel testimony here. I hope you are encouraged by it.

In July of 2001, I was at an *End Time Handmaiden's and Servant's of the Lord World Convention* when I had an unexpected visitation of angels. This visitation was a prophetic picture of what would happen in my ministry, *Glorious Creations*, in the future.

It happened on one of the first nights of the convention. Our hostess, Sister Gwen Shaw, shared during the worship time that she saw angels of the Lord walking among us. They had gifts in their hands. She asked that we join her in a corporate prayer of thanksgiving for what they would bring to us individually, according to what the Lord had for each of us.

I was waiting in an attitude of praise and thanksgiving, while at the same time not really expecting to see anything. I had dismissed the thought of receiving anything from an angel. Suddenly, in the spirit I saw an angel approach me. He was standing right in front of me and he had a smile on his face. I responded with a smile, that was most likely a cross between disbelief and curiosity at the same time.

He looked to be about 6'2". He had dark brown hair and blue eyes. Other than his clothing, he looked like a natural man that you might see anywhere. He was wearing a white robe that had a blue sash tied around his waist as a belt. He extended his right hand towards me. In his hand he held a clear plastic bag. It looked like a quart sized Ziploc bag. I couldn't tell what was in the bag; it was a dark substance that looked like it might be dirt. He extended his hand, as if to hand me the bag.

I didn't extend my hand to take it from him. I spoke out loud, even though I wasn't sure if I was seeing him in the physical or in the spirit. I told him that I couldn't accept the bag until I had asked the Holy Spirit if He wanted me to have it.

He backed away a step or two, bowed at the waist, with a smile on his face and instantly disappeared. I asked the Holy Spirit to tell me if He wanted me to accept the bag. I also repented and asked forgiveness for refusing it, if I had offended the Lord by refusing the gift. The Holy Spirit said that He was pleased that I sought Him before accepting the package from the heavenly being.

I don't want you to think that I didn't trust the Conference host's word as being from the Lord, but I was mature enough to know to always seek the Lord first, no matter how the supernatural appearance might look. The issue should never be about the gift, but the question should be asked if it is from God, our God. The Word says that satan can disguise himself as an angel of light, so we must always test the spirits.

Since this encounter, I have asked angels that have appeared to me if they can agree that Jesus is Lord, and they smile and nod their agreement. This is important information for these end days, as the Bible says there will be lying signs and wonders.

2 Thessalonians 2:9 says,

The coming of the lawless one will be accompanied by the working of satan with every kind of power, sign, and false wonder. (ESV)

The other thing that certainly had an impact on the decision to not take the bag of dirt until asking the Lord about it, was my view of angels and their ministry on the earth at that time.

When this vision occurred, I was concerned about the current trend of what appeared to be angel worship. At that time there were many people filling their homes with statues and pictures of angels. I know when someone starts to collect something in particular, it seems everyone wants to buy that for them for every occasion. I am not judging a person who has a home full of angel statues and pictures of them on their walls, but they need to examine the decorating from the perspective of the Lord and His angels. They shouldn't want their home to become a shrine for angels, with no glory given to the Lord in the home.

The Holy Spirit said that I was to take the bag, so I asked Him to send the angel back. Later that night I had a dream. In the dream, the angel came with the bag of dirt in his hand.

I thanked him and reached for the bag. But as I reached for it, he laid the bag down on the floor at my feet. As he did this, it turned into a larger bag. It looked like a sand bag about two feet long and a foot and a half wide. As he turned to leave, I saw that there were many more angels behind him. Each one had a large bag of dirt in their hands. These bags looked like the first bag that he had laid on the floor in front to me. All the angels had smiles on their faces as they kept piling the bags up in front of me.

When the bags of dirt were piled to about 8-10 feet high, I threw my hand up in the air and said, "Stop. I don't know what to do with all of this dirt! I have to ask the Lord about this." They all stopped, nodded to me and left.

The next morning in worship as I was thinking about the dream, the hostess said that there were people there who had received visions and didn't understand what the Lord was saying to them. She referred anyone who had questions about the angels to speak to a certain retired pastor who was at the meeting. She explained that he had been experiencing visitations of angels for about seven years at that time.

I certainly had questions that needed answers. I thought these bags of dirt must have something to do with the International Ministry of the Handmaidens, and the Lord had something for me to do with the ministry. I went to visit the pastor and told him my dream.

After listening to the story, the pastor said that he believed the bags of dirt were fertile soil that represented the lives of people that the Lord was going to bring to me. I wouldn't have to try to find people, but God would send forth His angels and they would bring the fertile soil right to me to be ministered to. The pastor saw an angel on either side of me holding a golden mantle on my shoulders, representing the ministry that the Lord had called me to. He didn't know what the ministry was, but from the amount of soil that I had seen, it seemed that the Lord would use our ministry to effect many lives in a mighty way.

That evening during our time of worship, the Lord opened my spiritual eyes again. I was standing facing the large wall of the bags of soil, when suddenly the first angel stepped through the bags and stood in front of me looking into my eyes with a smile on his face. He had a large sword in his hand. He handed it to me and motioned to me to open the first bag of soil with the sword. I looked down and saw the first bag that he had laid at my feet. I took the sword and made a movement as if I was slicing open the bag.

This was all done in the spiritual realm. Suddenly, as I completed the movement in the spirit, I could see the bag lay open and there was soil all around my feet and I was standing in the middle of it. Then I saw other angels begin to come through the bags of soil, form a circle around me, and begin to perform an Israeli folk dance. Then the vision ended. I am writing this in 2020. It is 19 years later, and this encounter is still as fresh in my mind as if it were yesterday.

I kept pondering the meaning of the vision. I did know that it had to do with the ministry while at the Handmaidens' Convention, but in what capacity? I asked the Lord about this. The next morning as I was opening up my table in the Marketplace, the Holy Spirit spoke to my heart and said, "The first bag of soil that you cut open with the sword will be soil that I will send to you right here at your table, and you will know that your vision has been from Me."

The Lord went on to say, "Plant the information that I have given you about the worship items into the fertile soil that I will send to your booth." I began to praise the Lord for the soil that He was sending.

To add a little information, this was on Friday, and we had been with our Glorious Creations booth since the Sunday before. We were selling worship items, flags, streamers and glory hoops. But not one of the worship instruments called a tabret had sold, which was very unusual. I couldn't understand this because usually everyone loves and buys the tabrets. They are beautiful and, as all of our other items, they come with scriptural validation paperwork and the effect that is felt in the spiritual realm when you use them.

As I was removing the cover from our tables, people began to come to our booth and ask me to explain the purpose of the tabrets. I explained about the tabrets and the impact that they made in the heavenly realm when we use them in praise, worship and intercession. The Lord continued to send more people and they were all asking and listening as I explained about the tabrets. We sold out of the tabrets that morning as a testimony to the Lord.

The story continues......

I had been home about two weeks, when in prayer one morning I thought about those bags of soil. I asked the Lord to send me another bag, and that I would be faithful to sow what He had given me.

Suddenly, an angel who looked like the same one I had seen before, was standing in front of me in my living room with a bag of soil in his hands. He laid it down on the floor and bowed and smiled. I thanked him and He disappeared.

I thanked the Lord for the soil and asked Him what I should do with it. Then the phone rang. It was a man who identified himself as Pastor Thomas Smith Kudjoe from Ghana, West Africa. He said that a Messianic Pastor had anointed him with oil and prayed over him and blew a shofar over him. Immediately the Holy Spirit spoke to him and told him to study about the spiritual significance of the blowing of the shofar and then to preach on it.

As he studied, he found out when you blow a shofar it is considered the shout of the Lord. He called it his 'shout message.' He referenced the story about Joshua marching around the walls of Jerico with the priests going ahead of them blowing on the shofars. On the seventh day the walls fell down flat. He shared the story of Gideon with his torch in one hand and shofar in the other and his shout.

During the week ahead of preaching about the shout of the Lord, his father had a stroke and was in the hospital in poor condition. After preaching his message about the shofar, the Holy Spirit spoke to him to take the shofar to the hospital and to blow it over his father. He was so excited. He said that as he blew the shofar and praised the Lord, his father was healed. They agreed to discharge him from the hospital that afternoon. He was in church that very night.

The pastor said that he began to read everything he could in the scriptures about the shofar. Then he searched on the computer to find someone who taught on this subject. He found our web site and called with questions.

He said that his people needed to know this important information, along with more about Israel. I had been to Israel several times and also had a history of Israeli folk dancing that he wanted his people to learn more about. He told me that he wanted to know my schedule because he was going to come to the United States to attend a conference so he could learn more. After that we prayed together on the phone and during the prayer the Holy Spirit spoke to me and said that I was to go there! I was shocked to hear that. I had never had any desire to go to Africa. I told him what the Lord had said to me and he immediately extended an invitation. I told him I would run it by my husband and some others I usually prayed with. I told him if I did come to Africa I would bring a group. He said that would be great.

After I finished talking with him, I was praying and seeking the Lord when the angel appeared again, and he had the large sword in his hand. The Holy Spirit said "You asked for another bag of soil; now it is time to open it." The angel extended the sword he was holding and I took it from him.

I raised the sword above my head (I physically acted it out). As I was bringing the sword down on the bag of soil (which was invisible to my physical eyes, but was visible with my spiritual eyes) a very loud, forceful shout like the sound of a shofar came out of my mouth. As the sword cut through the bag of soil, in the spirit I saw the bag split open. It was full of black rich dirt. There was a force that came out of me when I opened the bag. That force threw me physically backwards about three feet and I landed on the couch. I took this to mean this was a confirmation that I was to go to Africa. I opened my Bible and, as if by itself, it turned to Judges 6:34: *But the Spirit of the Lord clothed Gideon with Himself and took possession of him, and he blew a trumpet, and Abiezer was gathered to him.* The root word for *trumpet* in this scripture is 'rams horn' which is a shofar.

Within six months of opening the bag I did go to Africa, along with a team of 15 people. God gave us many signs and wonders on that trip. I have written about it in the book I wrote called From *God's Hands To Your Land—Blessings.*

That first trip was in 2002, and it began a relationship with that pastor and his family and the church family in Tema, Ghana that has developed over the years. We travel back and forth to share with those who have now become our family. The pastor is now a bishop. When he and family travel to the U.S., they usually try to include a stay with us.

I know this story sounds farfetched to some, but God has provided much proof that it really did happen and continues to happen. It is all due to His continuing mission for my life. I didn't ask for the angels, and I don't expect them when they show up.

All of these years, angels have been coming with bags of fertile soil. I get a call to speak somewhere, and the Lord confirms that is where I am to go. These stories may someday become a book of my adventures to many different states and nations throughout these years since I first saw the angels in 2001.

Test the Spirits/Angels

According to scripture it is important to test the spirits. Many people are asking God to open their eyes to see angels. So it is important to know what the scripture has to say about angelic visitations.

> *Beloved, do not believe every spirit [speaking through a self-proclaimed prophet]; instead test the spirits to see whether they are from God, because many false pro-phets and teachers have gone out into the world. By this you know and recognize the Spirit of God: every spirit*

that acknowledges and confesses [the fact] that Jesus Christ has [actually] come in the flesh [as a man] is from God [God is its source]; and every spirit that does not confess Jesus [acknow-ledging that He has come in the flesh, but would deny any of the Son's true nature] is not of God; this is the spirit of the antichrist, which you have heard is coming, and is now already in the world.
1 John 4:1-3

Angels can speak, so they can profess Jesus or they can assure you in some way that the Lord is their God. If they don't affirm that Jesus is Lord, they aren't from God.

Chapter 10

What Kind of People Are Prophetic Intercessors?

We see from some stories in the Bible that prophetic intercession isn't restricted only to those who have years of intercessory prayer experience. The Lord doesn't have a long list of qualifications. There isn't any recipe to follow that will turn you into a prophetic intercessor, but there are certain things you can do that will help you create the right atmosphere, within yourself and around you, that will welcome and even encourage the Holy Spirit to operate through you in this way.

You start by reading the Word and meditating on what it is saying to you. Spend quiet time listening to worship music, stilling your spirit so you can hear the Lord speak or give you an impression in your mind while in that atmosphere. Pray unceasingly, as Paul says in the New Testament. That doesn't mean you are praying out loud all of the time, but you can be praying in the spirit silently as you go about your day, listening to what the Holy Spirit is saying to you as you interact with different people and situations.

If you are one who has been chosen by God for this type of intercession, then you would be described as a person who is spiritually hungry to understand the deeper mysteries of the Spirit. The Word says you would be *apostolic* in nature, a forerunner, and a spiritual treasure hunter—led of the Holy Spirit. You would be a visionary person in nature, willing to

135

make yourself available for the Lord to use to see His purposes fulfilled on the earth. You might be very creative and want to create prophetic items to worship the Lord with.

Most dictionaries say *apostolic* means 'one sent on a mission.' So if you have an apostolic anointing you will love to travel. You might feel led of the Holy Spirit to travel to a particular city and perform a prophetic act for the Lord, even without anyone else knowing about it. The point is you are always ready to go and do what He says.

If you have an apostolic call on your life, the Bible says there are signs and wonders that indicate a genuine apostle. Paul says:

> *And my message and my preaching were not in persuasive words of wisdom (using clever rehtoric) but (they were delivered) in demonstration of the (Holy) Spirit (operating through me) and of (His) power (stirring and minds of listeners and persuading them. 1 Corinthians 2:4*

> *The signs that indicate a genuine apostle were performed among you and most patiently —signs and wonders and miracles. 2 Corinthians 12:12*

This is not to say a person has to be considered an apostle to be used of the Lord. God uses everyone who believes in Him to bring His glory to the earth. It is just a clear explanation of what a true apostle is. Contrary to some opinions, all the offices of the fivefold ministry are still in operation and will be until Jesus returns. These offices are found in Ephesians 4:11.

And [His gifts to the church were varied and] He Himself appointed some as apostles [special messengers, representatives], some as prophets [who speak a new message from God to the people], some as evangelists [who spread the good news of salvation], and some as pastors and teachers [to shepherd and guide and instruct].

A person can be considered both apostolic and prophetic. As apostolic prophetic people, we soon discover that prophetic acts are already a normal part of our lives. We don't have to be in the office of prophet to prophecy or move in a prophetic manner. Often others will recognize the call on a person's life before the person himself does.

Prayers that draw God's attention.

The Word gives us an example of how our prayers on the earth draw the attention of the Lord. We read that there are some qualities that a prophetic intercessor exhibits that will cause God to hear his prayers and respond.

In Caesarea there was a man named Cornelius, a centurion of the Italian Cohort, as it was called. He was a devout man who feared God with all his household; he gave alms generously to the people and prayed constantly to God. One afternoon at about three o'clock he had a vision in which he clearly saw an angel of God coming in and saying to him, "Cornelius." He stared at him in terror and said, "What is it, Lord?" He answered, "Your prayers and your alms have ascended as a memorial before God.   Acts 10:1-6 NRSV

As we walk to the best of our ability in an attitude of humility and with personal integrity, we will also draw God's attention to our prayers. This isn't to say our whole family has to be walking in righteousness, but God will increase our anointing and his draw upon them as we live rightly before Him. As we go about God's business He will take care of ours.

As intercessors, one of the first things we learn is that our intercession isn't about us, it is about God and His purposes. What He tells us to do or say might not come at a convenient time for us. In most of the examples we read about in the Bible, we see that God didn't seem to consider how the person was feeling at the moment He gave them an assignment to perform.

To some, prophetic intercessors fit into the heading of 'peculiar people.' We are a unique group and at times can seem pretty peculiar. God desires to use each of as glory carriers to bring heaven to earth. The Lord searches for those who consider themselves to be ordinary people to use to change the world.

> But ye are a chosen generation, a royal priesthood, a holy nation, a peculiar people; that ye should shew forth the Praise of Him who hath called you out of darkness into His marvelous light.
> 1 Peter 2:9 KJV

Intercessors enjoy the benefit of dual citizenship

Most prophetic intercessors are aware of the fact that they have a dual citizenship, which means they are citizens of two worlds.

Jesus was talking about believers when He said,

138

"I have given to them Your word [the message You gave Me]; and the world has hated them because they are not of the world and do not belong to the world, just as I am not of the world and do not belong to it. I do not ask You to take them out of the world, but that You keep them and protect them from the evil one. They are not of the world, just as I am not of the world. Sanctify them in the truth [set them apart for Your purposes, make them holy]; Your word is truth. John 17:14-17

Prophetic intercessors understand that even though they were physically born here on earth, after accepting Jesus as their Savior they experience a spiritual new birth and became citizens of a spiritual kingdom which is called the Kingdom of Heaven or the Kingdom of God. This new birth experience is a Kingdom mystery that is an amazing experience. In this story Jesus explains the mystery of being "born again,"

Now there was a certain man among the Pharisees named Nicodemus, a ruler (member of the Sanhedrin) among the Jews, who came to Jesus at night and said to Him, "Rabbi (Teacher), we know [without any doubt] that You have come from God as a teacher; for no one can do these signs [these wonders, these attesting miracles] that You do unless God is with him."

Jesus answered him, "I assure you and most solemnly say to you, unless a person is born again [reborn from above—spiritually transformed, renewed, sanctified], he cannot [ever] see and experience the kingdom of God."

Nicodemus said to Him, "How can a man be born when he is old? He cannot enter his mother's womb a second time and be born, can he?" Jesus answered, "I assure you and most solemnly say to you, unless one is born of water and the Spirit he cannot [ever] enter the kingdom of God. That which is born of the flesh is flesh [the physical is merely physical], and that which is born of the Spirit is spirit. Do not be surprised that I have told you, 'You must be born again [reborn from above—spiritually transformed, renewed, sanctified].' The wind blows where it wishes and you hear its sound, but you do not know where it is coming from and where it is going; so it is with everyone who is born of the Spirit." John 3:1-8

When a person becomes born again into the Kingdom of God, they immediately become an eligible candidate for this prophetic prayer ministry. Usually a person follows a road of progression that leads to maturity in the symbolic prophetic ministry, although that isn't something that is always predictable.

For we are His workmanship [His own master work, a work of art], created in Christ Jesus [reborn from above—spiritually transformed, renewed, ready to be used] for good works, which God prepared [for us] beforehand [taking paths which He set], so that we would walk in them [living the good life which

He prearranged and made ready for us].
Ephesians 2:10

Believers have citizenship in two kingdoms.

Just as the two kingdoms have their names, they each have a description of how they operate. In the kingdom known as *earth,* in America, we live in what is called a democracy. A democracy is a government in which the supreme power is held by the people and used by them directly or indirectly through representation. Synonyms of *democracy* are republic, self-government, self-rule.

The Kingdom of God is a theocracy which is a system of government in which a religious body holds unlimited power. Under a theocracy, an entire nation officially follows one religion. Jesus is our King. He is the head over our theocratic government which is also known as the Kingdom of God or the Kingdom of Heaven.

> *And [so that you will begin to know] what the immeasurable and unlimited and surpassing greatness of His [active, spiritual] power is in us who believe. These are in accordance with the working of His mighty strength, which He produced in Christ when He raised Him from the dead and seated Him at His own right hand in the heavenly places, far above all rule ad authority and power and dominion [whether angelic or human], and [far above] every name that is named [above every title that can be conferred], not only in this age and world but also in the one to come. And He put all things [in every realm] in subjection under Christ's feet, and appointed Him as [supreme and*

141

*authoritative] head over all things in the church.
Ephesians 1:19-22*

*For you are a holy people [set apart] to the LORD
your God; and the LORD has chosen you out of all
the peoples who are on the earth to be a people
for His own possession.   Deuteronomy 14:2*

As citizens of the Kingdom of God, we are ambassadors of
the Lord who are to perform His wishes here on earth.

Spiritually birthing God's purposes on the earth.

The following scripture speaks of birthing in the Spirit.

*Flesh gives birth to flesh, but the Spirit gives birth
to spirit. John 3:6*

Only the Holy Spirit can bring about a spiritual birthing. It is
completely foreign for our flesh to understand.

You may have never witnessed a person going through the
process of a spiritual birthing, or you may have personally
experienced birthing a spiritual baby. Every intercessor
needs to be acquainted with this subject.

Whether you are experienced in this aspect of prophetic
intercession or not, doesn't seem to make a difference to
the Lord. If you are willing, He may use you in this way.

The Holy Spirit may reveal that you are carrying a spiritual
seed that will develop into a 'spiritual baby'. Or He may
reveal that a seed was sown some time in your past and has
developed into a spiritual baby that you will be able to bring
to birth in its proper time.

An example of a spiritual baby is a vision that the Lord has
given a person something He desires them to accomplish in

their lifetime. Maybe He has planted in them a vision of writing a book or going on a mission trip. He may have given them a word about moving to another location.

It doesn't have to be something that we feel would shake the nations. It can be anything that God has planted in a person's heart that hasn't come to fruition. It may not seem important to the person, but it is to God. We never know if it is an important part of a puzzle God is working on that could affect cities, states, or even nations.

God's timing isn't the same in the spirit as it is on the earth. In the physical birthing process, we know that a regular pregnancy takes approximately nine months from conception to the birth.

The following testimony addresses spiritual timing as it pertains to spiritual birthing. I was at a conference and witnessed a woman give birth to a 'spiritual baby.' She gave her testimony concerning the birthing of this spiritual baby. She said that she was given a vision 50 years earlier, when she was a young girl attending a church youth group. She saw herself on a mission trip.

As years passed, she gradually forgot about the vision. But when the teaching on spiritual birthing began that day, she began to feel a stirring in her belly which turned into birthing pains. She birthed a baby that day and the Holy Spirit told her that its name was *missions*.

She told us that she had recently been thinking about going on her first mission trip with her church but had forgotten about the vision God had given her 50 years earlier. God didn't forget!

*But you must not forget this one thing, dear
friends: A day is like a thousand years to the Lord,
and a thousand years is like a day. 2 Peter 3:8 NLT*

Don't limit God.

Sometimes a person receives a prophetic word spoken over
them at a time when the fulfillment seems impossible. They
put it out of their mind, but God hasn't put it out of His
mind. If the person is willing, he will bring it to pass.

A spiritual seed can get planted in any number of ways: a
dream, vision, prophetic word, or a word of knowledge
spoken over a person. If the person thinks it is something
that they won't be able to do because they limit themselves
and God, then He will find someone else to bring it to birth
even though they are His first choice.

There is an example of this in the book of Esther.

Esther has been chosen by God to save the Jews. She
couldn't imagine God would use her since she was an
orphan and was very humble. The truth was that her destiny
had been laid out for her many years before so God's
purposes for the nation of Israel would be fulfilled through
her actions.

Her uncle, Mordecai, knows that she may be uncertain
about doing what God has called her to do. He thinks it is a
very real possibility that she thinks it is too much for her to
do, and if what she was to do didn't work, it could cost her
life. Mordecai encourages her by sending her this answer.

*Do not think that because you are in the king's
house you alone of all the Jews will escape. For if
you remain silent at this time, relief and*

144

deliverance for the Jews will arise from another place, but you and your father's family will perish. And who knows but that you have come to your royal position for such a time as this?"
Esther 4:13-14 AMP.

Because Esther did what was asked of her even though she didn't feel she could, God used her to birth something new – freedom for the whole Jewish nation.

Spiritual birthing can and usually does come as quite a surprise.

But just as it is written in scripture "Things which the eye has not seen and the ear has not heard, And which have not entered the heart of man, all that God has prepared for those who love Him [who hold Him in affectionate reverence, who obey Him, and who gratefully recognize the benefits that He has bestowed]." For God has unveiled them and revealed them to us through the [Holy] Spirit; for the Spirit searches all things [diligently], even [sounding and measuring] the [profound] depths of God [the divine counsels and things far beyond human understanding]. 1 Corinthians 2:9-10

Spiritual birthing isn't limited to a woman. Both men and women can carry and spiritually birth the purposes of God. Just as a woman can be impregnated and carry a human baby to full term, a man or woman can be impregnated with a spiritual seed of destiny and carry a spiritual baby, and birth it into the physical earthly realm, fulfilling a mission from heaven.

The Lord Himself spiritually birthed Israel in a day. This happened in the physical but was prophesied spiritually many years earlier.

> *"Who has heard of such a thing? Who has seen such things? Can a land be born in one day? Or can a nation be brought forth in a moment? As soon as Zion was in labor, she also brought forth her sons.*
> *Isaiah 66:8*

Never in the history of the world had such a thing happened before—but God keeps His word. As foretold here and in Ezekiel 37:21-22, Israel became a recognized nation, actually "born in one day." After being away from their homeland for almost 2,000 years, the Jews were given a national homeland in Palestine by the Balfour Declaration in November 1917. In 1922, the League of Nations gave Great Britain the mandate over Palestine. On May 14, 1948, Great Britain withdrew her mandate, and immediately Israel was declared a sovereign state, and her growth and importance among nations was astonishing.

What the physical manifestation of a spiritual birthing looks like.

The manifestations that I have seen and experienced of spiritual birthing over the past 40 years all seem to follow the same course. The only difference is in the way a person handles it.

Just as in a natural birth, there are some who go through spiritual birthing calmly and without a lot of noise. There are others who scream, cry, yell, and scare others, and themselves.

Of course, if a person doesn't know what is happening to them it may be a valid fear. But if I am the one assisting, I tell the person that they don't need to scream. I calmly explain to them what is happening.

When the Holy Spirit begins to move on a person in the spiritual birthing process, they will begin to feel something physical happening to them. Usually it starts with some pain in their stomach. Most women will say it is a pain that feels like contractions starting. Men usually say it feels like a bad stomachache. The pain-like contractions will intensify as in a natural birth. Soon, the person is doubled over and maybe lying on the floor moaning and groaning. This could be likened to a type of travailing. During the whole birthing process, the person birthing can communicate just like a woman who is going through real labor.

In the beginning of the process, there will be a pause of time between the contractions just as there is in real labor. That is the time to move the person out of the way of everyone, if it is needed. Assure the person that they can get up and move with assistance. If they refuse, cover them with something for privacy reasons. Explain to those who might not know what is happening, that the person is birthing a spiritual baby. You can coach the person birthing and explain to them what is going on (if they don't know) which will calm them down.

I have seen people rush to the side of someone who is birthing and begin to call out demons and try to deliver them. This is a possibility. Demons can manifest too and confuse people. Don't be afraid to ask the person if the Lord is delivering them of something or if they are birthing a baby. This is a valid question, and the one birthing should be able to answer you clearly.

The birthing will reach a point when the person who is birthing won't be paying attention to anything going on around them, and they will say they feel the urge to push just as if they are birthing a baby.

Some people may say their back is hurting. Ask them if you can rub their back. If they let you, it will help them. It seems the process of the birthing is generally 20-30 minutes, sometimes less. When the birthing process is over the person will stop feeling the urge to push. They seem to go limp. They will be able to tell you if the birthing is complete.

Instruct them to ask the Lord the name of the baby they have just birthed. He will assuredly give them a name. When they have rested, they need to lift this spiritual baby up to the Lord and thank Him for it and make a declaration of dedication to do their best to raise this baby, which may be a ministry or particular assignment God is giving them.

Sometimes the person will collapse again, or may not even get up from the first birthing, and another baby comes. They birth twins. They should follow the same process for the second baby as the first. I have witnessed a woman birth twins and their names were Unity and Freedom. She said she had been interceding for unity among the churches and freedom from spiritual bondage for the people in the region for a long time.

Some people have told me that they have been carrying a spiritual baby for years, waiting for God's timing to birth it. They didn't understand what was happening to them, but they knew something was up, and they felt pregnant.

A person may feel some contractions, but nothing more occurs. Most likely they will birth at another time. The Holy Spirit is giving them a sign that they are carrying a spiritual baby.

Does a person always have to go through the physical manifestations to spiritually birth a baby? The answer is no. I don't know why God chooses to do it this way at times. A person can birth new things spiritually in the physical realm and not go through this process. They might have a sense inside of them that something has just been birthed and can ask the Lord what is it, and then decree what the Holy Spirit tells them to. If God chooses to birth a spiritual baby through you or someone you are with, understanding this process will help you to be better equipped to know what is happening and how to handle it.

Intercessors are watchmen gatekeepers.

I will stand at my guard post and station myself on the tower; and I will keep watch to see what he will say to me, and what answer I will give (as his spokesman) when I am reproved. Habakkuk 2:1

The wording in this scripture points out that an intercessor is a watchman. The intercessor/watchman receives a word from the Lord and writes it down. As watchmen, intercessors learn to keep secrets the Lord speaks to them until the right time to reveal His word.

If you are excited about what the Lord is doing with you and share with those who don't understand, they may talk about you behind your back. This would be considered judging and gossip by the Lord, and the accuser uses it to provide an open door to get a judgment from God against the person who is doing the judging.

We see an example of this in Numbers 12:1-9.

> Now Miriam and Aaron spoke against Moses because of the Cushite woman whom he had married (for he had married a Cushite woman);and they said, "Has the Lord really spoken only through Moses? Has He not spoken also through us?" And the Lord heard it. Now the man Moses was very humble (gentle, kind, devoid of self-righteousness), more than any man who was on the face of the earth.)

> Suddenly the Lord said to Moses, Aaron, and Miriam, "Come out, you three, to the Tent of Meeting (tabernacle)." And the three of them came out. The Lord came down in a pillar of cloud and stood at the doorway of the tabernacle, and He called Aaron and Miriam, and they came forward. And He said, "Hear now My words: If there is a prophet among you, I the Lord will make myself known to him in a vision. I will speak to him in a dream. "but it is not so with my servant Moses; he is entrusted and faithful in all My house. With him I speak mouth to mouth [directly], Clearly and openly and not in riddles; And he beholds the form of the Lord.

> Why then were you not afraid to speak against My servant Moses?" And the anger of the Lord was kindled against Miriam and Aaron, and He departed. But when the cloud had withdrawn from

*over the tent, behold, Miriam was leprous, as white
as snow. And Aaron turned and looked at Miriam,
and, behold, she was leprous.*

Miriam is presumed to be the leader of the attack on Moses'
authority because she is mentioned before Aaron, and
because of the severity of her punishment. This is the first
recorded judgment of God due to gossip. The judgment was
the curse of leprosy, which is a skin disease.

Not everyone who suffers from a skin disease is under
judgment for gossip or criticizing someone. There is a
possibility that it comes from a generational curse,
especially if it shows up on a baby or a child.

If it is due to a curse, then repentance and forgiveness could
take care of it. I am not ruling out other causes—just giving
some suggestions of things to cover in the spiritual realm.

*Do not judge or you too will be judged. For in the
same way you judge another, you will be judged,
and with the measure you use, it will be measured
to you.   Matthew 7:1 NIV*

If the Lord gives you an assignment and you share it with
the wrong person or people, the enemy may use them to
turn on you and spread information that shouldn't be
shared, and it may not even be true.

Some things are meant to be between the Lord and you. If
you want to share your exploits, or what the Lord is
speaking to you, then find like-minded people to share with.
Take care not to judge anyone who doesn't understand you.

You can get in trouble or cause problems for your pastor if
others are talking about you. This could result in the enemy

causing everything to be put into confusion, and you may not be able to accomplish your mission.

Even when you are used by the Lord to operate as a prophetic intercessor, it is easy to sometimes get annoyed by other people who seem to be bragging about what the Lord is asking them to do, their exploits, and how He is talking to them. They may be totally innocent of how others perceive them and don't realize how they sound to others. They are just excited to be hearing from God. If you are in a position to advise them at all, you should do so in a loving way so they don't go through unnecessary rejection from those who don't understand their enthusiasm because God doesn't speak to them in the same way.

You will have opportunity to share when you get with likeminded believers who also have testimonies they want to share. This is great training for when the Lord has you do something undercover. You have already disciplined yourself to keep it to yourself.

Remember what happened to Sampson when he revealed the secret of his strength to Delilah. He had a warning from God to keep this secret, but in a moment of weakness he divulged the secret and became a slave to his enemies. (see Judges 16) We have to be wise not foolish, and learn to keep secrets that He shares with us. It is normal to want to have God share His secrets with us as intercessors. He says in His Word that He will.

One of the reasons it is sometimes best not share with people who are not part of your team is because, as we read examples of prophetic intercession in the Word, it becomes obvious very quickly that prophetic intercessors cannot depend on human thinking or reasoning.

What if a person isn't interested in prophetic intercession?

There are some people who aren't interested in this type of ministry. That's ok. The Lord will lead them to operate in the other gifts in their lives. God knows who is and who isn't interested. He is the one who calls each person and anoints them with their specific anointings to fulfill their purposes in the Kingdom.

Activate yourself

No matter what stage of life you are in or what your spiritual upbringing has been, I hope you have found information that is an asset to you in your walk as a believer. I pray that as you have read this book it has been a call to action in your life, and your spiritual vision has been enhanced, and that you are better able to relate to the value of the use of prophetic intercession. If you are willing, extend your hand to the Lord and invite Him to intervene in your life. Step forward into history; be bold and courageous. As prophetic intercessors we will perform exploits for the Lord.

The people that do know their God shall be strong and do exploits. Daniel 11:32b KJV

You can decree this prophetic declaration over yourself or for anyone for whom you are standing in the gap.

Favor of God prophetic declaration

The favor of God surrounds me as a shield, it goes before me to support, endorse, and strengthen me. Through my God, I am fearless and full of faith. Lord, Your hand of blessing is upon me. Your favor will cause doors to open before me and add great blessings in my life, to the point that it is noticeable as a witness to others. I will fulfill all of Your purposes for my life. I decree all of this in the name of Jesus. Amen.

(Psalm 5:12; Psalm139:5; Isaiah 41:10; Psalm 115:14; Revelation 3:8; 2 Corinthians 2:8)

About the Author

Hello. I am Jeanette Strauss.

In 1997, my husband, Bud and I founded and are the co-owners of Glorious Creations. Glorious Creations is a Worship and Praise adornment company. You can learn more about that by going to our website. www.gloriouscreations.net

I am ordained as a minister through Gospel Crusade and have been in full time ministry since 1998.

My husband and I are active members of New Heart Ministries in Coldwater, Michigan. I am an active member of Aglow International speaking in many Aglow conferences. I am an active intercessor for Southwest Michigan under the Regional leadership of Dr. Douglas Carr and the state leadership of Barbara Yoder of Breakthrough Apostolic Ministries (BAM). I am a member intercessor for Heartland Apostolic Prayer Network (HAPN) for Michigan under the leadership of Anita Christopher.

If you would be interested in having me come and share about this subject of Prophetic Intercession or any of the other books I have written, you can contact me through our website or email me at: jeanette@gloriouscreations.net, or call our office at 517-639-4395.

Cover art by James Nesbit

Overseer of *Prepare the Way Ministries International.* James has been used by God to help prepare the way for the coming awakening in America through strategic level intercessory assignments. He has unique insight and understanding. He is overseer of *Mountain Alliance of Illinois,* HAPN and RPN state coordinator for Illinois, and overseer for the region named Joy Number Nine, which includes the states of Missouri, Kentucky, Illinois, Indiana, Ohio, and Michigan.

James also has a strong prophetic art mantle resting upon his life. He believes prophetic artists have a Habakkuk 2:2 assignment to write the vision and make it plain so the body can quickly understand it and run with the word of the Lord. As the old saying goes, "A picture is worth a thousand words." Peter Wagner and Cindy Jacobs have proclaimed him one of the leading prophetic artists in the earth today. The Lord has seen fit to allow his artwork to be displayed in many nations throughout the earth.

Visit the online gallery at www.jamesnart.com. James can also be reached through www.ptwministries.com or nesb7@aol.com.

Other resources from Jeanette Strauss
To order call (517) 639-4395
www.gloriouscreations.net

Heavenly Impact Symbolic Praise, Worship, and Intercession
"On Earth As It Is In Heaven"

This book is a must read for those seeking a Biblical foundation for the use of symbolic tools of praise, worship and intercession. This information presents clear guidelines concerning their proper place and use.

Explore the Possibilities! *Heavenly Impact* guides you through Bible history and explains the relevance of worship adornment as it identifies strategic value to worship. Scripture references reveal that our actions on earth truly do have a "Heavenly Impact".

Tools covered: flags, billows, Mat-teh', shofar, streamers, tabrets, and veils, vocabulary of movement and Biblical color symbolism. Also available in Spanish. $14.00

Heavenly Impact—Teaching Bundle

This bundle includes a Teachers Manual and Student Workbook great for teaching Dance Ministry or Small Life Groups.

The Teachers Manual includes Prophetic Activations and Exercises at the end of the chapters and different discussion topics.

Each chapter includes the questions, along with the answers, for the teacher's convenience and references the page the answer is on in the *Heavenly Impact* book.

The Student Workbook includes the questions, prophetic activations and exercises, and a section of biblical significance of colors.

Included is a "Certificate Of Completion" suitable for framing. Set includes one *Heavenly Impact*, one Teachers Manual, one Student Manual, and one Certificate of Completion. $40.00

From the Courtroom of Heaven to the Throne of Grace and Mercy

This a revised and expanded version of the *Courtroom of Heaven Book*. It includes more examples of scriptures and testimonies that will encourage you as you present your case in the Heavenly Court in front of the Righteous Judge. As a born again Christian, I had never given the Courtroom of Heaven a thought. Then in answer to a prayer my husband and I prayed in 2005 for our daughter, who had backslidden from her faith in Jesus, the Lord gave me a dream.

The dream contained a strategy to use in the Courtroom of Heaven on her behalf. As a result she was set free and restored. Included in this book is the dream, and the strategy that can be used to win your specific petition in the Heavenly Court. Show up where the accuser of the brethren does not expect you, and win your case! The prayer we prayed for our daughter is included in this book. You can pray it for anyone. Just put their name in the blank space provided and see how the Lord will work to move heaven and earth on their behalf. You will have results on earth as it is in heaven!- $14.00

Courtroom of Heaven – Prayers and Petitions

This is the companion book for the book *From the Courtroom of Heaven to the Throne of Grace and Mercy*. It contains many examples of Prayers and Petitions that a person can read and put a name in the blank space provided. These prayers and petitions pertain to individual cases or trials, spiritual or physical, that people may find themselves involved in. These prayers are in addition to the prayers found in the Courtroom book.

The prayers are Court Ready, Biblical prayers or petitions that you can read word for word. All you need to do is fill the names of the people who are involved in each particular case as you present it before the Righteous Judge of Heaven and Earth. Subjects covered: Presenting a Petition; Preparing For Your Court Appointment; A Prayer Of Cleansing; Seeking The Removal of a Generational Bloodline Curse.; Marriage Problems Petition; Healing The Brokenhearted; Future Spouse; Healing of Sickness; Deliverance From Addictions; Freedom From Depression; Prosperity In Business; Finding Your Destiny; Prayer For the Unsaved and Backslidden; Repent, Repent, Petiton, Praise.

Even though it is tempting to purchase this Petition book only, the Court Room book fully explains the protocol and scriptural validation of going into the Courtroom of Heaven and standing before the Judge who is the Creator of Heaven and earth to present your case. $13.00

Courtroom of Heaven Bundle

In this bundle you will receive both the *Courtroom of Heaven Book* and the *Prayers and Petition* books.

A flash drive that is included contains my personal outline that can be printed out.

I use this outline when I share about the *Courtroom of Heaven* in seminars. The flashdrive also contains a Powerpoint presentation which goes along with the easy to follow outline.

Also included is a DVD of Jeanette's teaching on the *Courtroom of Heaven.* This is a perfect addition for anyone desiring to teach on this subject. It is great for small group study or for teaching large groups. $50.00

Redeem Your Home

This book contains Biblical teaching about the necessity of spiritually cleansing your home, apartment or business. It includes step-by-step instructions with prayers to read that will insure the dedication of your home, apartment or business to the Lord. This insures the removal of any demonic presence that may be residing within it. Don't wait; set your home, apartment, business and family free today! We include a free sample of the Shalom Anointing Oil that is enough for anointing one home. $10.00.

Redeem Your Home
Book and Oil Bundle

This oil is a combination of olive oil from Israel and a Kosher wine which serves as a symbol of the Blood of Christ as the sacrificial lamb.

And the blood shall be to you for a token upon the houses where ye are: and when I see the blood, I will pass over you, and the plague shall not be upon you to destroy you, when I smite the land of Egypt. Exodus 12:13

This oil/wine combination is to be placed over the doorposts and lintels as a symbol of covenant for all the Heavenly Realm to see. The name of this wine is appropriately named "Shalom" which makes a prophetic statement over every room inside that you anoint and your outside door posts that is read loud and clear by the heavenly hosts—both sides. It says this home or business is under "Covenant Protection." Many of us are familiar with the Hebrew word *Shalom* which is taken from the root word *shalam*. This word also means, "peace," to be safe in mind, body or estate. It speaks of sense of completeness and inner tranquility. It includes nothing missing, nothing broken. The common western definition of peace is the absence of conflict or war, which can fit well with what we are using it for as we anoint our homes.

This bundle includes a larger bottle of the Shalom Anointing Oil that is enough for anointing ten homes. $18.00

From God's Hands to Your Land

The Bible establishes the spiritual relationship between God and his land. The Lord desires to pour out his blessings on your land, but scripture says that his blessings can be blocked.

The Lord, as the Owner of the original title deed of all real estate, gave us the responsibility to subdue and take dominion over the land.

Included in this book are step-by-step instructions for the Restoration Ceremony, with prayers and decrees to recite as you reconcile, and redeem your land that will ensure that His blessings will flow freely on your land with no hindrances. $10.00 Also available in Spanish.

From God's Hands to Your Land Blessings Kit

Redeem Your Land Kit. This kit comes with everything you need to pray for your land. It has the book " *From God's Hands To Your Land- Blessings*"

It comes with four mini communion sets that contain the bread and the juice for communion. Included in your kit are packets of milk and honey, anointing oil, and a packet of harvest seeds to prophetically plant for the prosperity of the land. It has a scroll that is a symbolic Title Deed you can fill out and claim the Prophetic name the Lord calls your property in the Heavenly Courts "Register of the Deeds office." The book will answer any questions you might have concerning why you would use these items when you pray for your land. The easy to understand Biblically based explanation have supporting scriptures included in the book that is included in the kit. It makes the perfect gift for someone who is moving into a new place, but is also essential for those who have lived at their address for many years. Many people have sent in testimonies about how their circumstances that were dire before they redeemed their land have all changed for the good!

The book includes a 15 minute ceremony to read as you pray over and redeem your land and bless it. Included are step by step prayers and scriptures to complete your land redemption scripturally. $20.00

Glorious Creations
1114 Robinson Road, Quincy, Michigan 49082
517-639-4395 www.gloriouscreations.net

ORDER FORM

Product	Price	Quantity		Total
Heavenly Advance	$14.00	x _____	=	_____
From God's Hand to Your Land	$10.00	x _____	=	_____
De las Manos de Dios a Tu Tierra	$10.00	x _____	=	_____
Bless Your Land Kit	$20.00	x _____	=	_____
Redeem Your Home	$10.00	x _____	=	_____
Redeem Your Home & Oil	$18.00	x _____	=	_____
From the Courtroom of Heaven	$14.00	x _____	=	_____
From the Courtroom of Heaven Prayers and Petitions	$13.00	x _____	=	_____
From the Courtroom of Heaven Teaching Bundle	$50.00	x _____	=	_____
Heavenly Impact	$14.00	x _____	=	_____
Impacto Divino	$14.00	x _____	=	_____
Heavenly Impact Teaching Bundle	$40.00	x _____	=	_____
Heavenly Impact Student Workbook	$13.00	x _____	=	_____
		Total due for Product		_____
		Shipping & Handling		_____
		Total Amount Due		_____

Shipping & Handling:

0-$9.95	$ 4.00
$10 - $19.95	$ 6.00
$20.00 - $39.95	$ 8.00
$40.00 and up	$10.00

We ship Priority Mail.

For international shipping,
email us at
www.gloriouscreations.net

Glorious Creations
1114 Robinson Road, Quincy, Michigan 49082
517-639-4395 www.gloriouscreations.net

ORDER FORM

Product	Price	Quantity		Total
Heavenly Advance	$14.00	x _____	=	_____
From God's Hand to Your Land	$10.00	x _____	=	_____
De las Manos de Dios a Tu Tierra	$10.00	x _____	=	_____
Bless Your Land Kit	$20.00	x _____	=	_____
Redeem Your Home	$10.00	x _____	=	_____
Redeem Your Home & Oil	$18.00	x _____	=	_____
From the Courtroom of Heaven	$14.00	x _____	=	_____
From the Courtroom of Heaven Prayers and Petitions	$13.00	x _____	=	_____
From the Courtroom of Heaven Teaching Bundle	$50.00	x _____	=	_____
Heavenly Impact	$14.00	x _____	=	_____
Impacto Divino	$14.00	x _____	=	_____
Heavenly Impact Teaching Bundle	$40.00	x _____	=	_____
Heavenly Impact Student Workbook	$13.00	x _____	=	_____
		Total due for Product		_____
		Shipping & Handling		_____
		Total Amount Due		_____

Shipping & Handling:

0-$9.95	$ 4.00
$10 - $19.95	$ 6.00
$20.00 - $39.95	$ 8.00
$40.00 and up	$10.00

We ship Priority Mail.

For international shipping,
email us at
www.gloriouscreations.net